MW01051036

Finding Arcadia:
Wisdom, Truth, and Love in the Classics

Paul Krause

Jess,
Another journey to thank
you for meeting a wandering
writer. It's always wonderful
to meet fellow writers when I'm
off the beaten path.

-Paul

Finding Arcadia:
Wisdom, Truth, and Love in the Classics

Paul Krause

Academica Press
Washington~London

Library of Congress Cataloging-in-Publication Data

Names: Krause, Paul (author)
Title: Finding arcadia : wisdom, truth, and love in the classics | Krause, Paul

Description: Washington : Academica Press, 2023. | Includes references.
Identifiers: LCCN 2023931828 | ISBN 9781680537147 (hardcover) |
9781680537161 (paperback) | 9781680537154 (e-book)

Dedication

To the Fortune Family and Donald Wilson
for the kindness they showed me when studying in London.

Contents

Acknowledgements

I first want to acknowledge Paul du Quenoy and the editors at Academica Press for helping to bring this work to fruition. I am also indebted to several editors for the years of writing for them and the freedom to reprint my essays in this volume, they include: Stephen Klugewicz, Jeff Bilbro, Lee Trepanier, and Erich Prince. Lastly, I want to acknowledge the gentle reader who has endeavored to pilgrimage through the classics with me. The reader is the most important reason why any writer writes.

Introduction

Don't Cancel the Classics

Do the ancient Greeks have anything left to tell us? Anyone who deals extensively in the humanities, and especially the classics, inevitably must ask themselves this question. Apart from being eclectic or a renaissance individual, if the Greeks have nothing important to teach us, why bother wrestling with them at all? That seems to be the new prevailing spirit, notwithstanding the iconoclastic attitudes to ban, or "exclude," anything from that critically endangered species classicist Bernard Knox called Dead White European males.

Greek literature is one of the triumphs of Western civilization—not merely because it is the seed of our literary garden but because it captures the tensions of the human struggle to find meaning in the cosmos and our place therein. Greek literature is the battlefield of our restless hearts seeking comfort and serenity in an often cold, dark, and pitiless world. Indeed, the entire dialectical movement of Greek literature is a working out of the moral cosmos and its relationship to the *polis*—or our civil and political life.

The Hesiodic Cosmos

The Greek cosmos is not, initially, moral. It is, however, filled with pathos. It matters not whether Hesiod composed his poem before or after Homer. Giambattista Vico, in my mind, conclusively shows that poetic metaphysics begins with the violence of the sublime. Hesiod's *Theogony* is the quintessential sublimely violent poem and, therefore, draws on a tradition much older than Homer. The work, as we know, is an account of the birth of the gods.

There are two lines of gods in the Greek cosmos. The first refers to the pre-existing gods of the pre-existent world, the primordial gods, who are not the product of sex. The second line of gods, the Titans and the Olympians, are the offspring of sex—and very violent sex. The Hesiodic cosmos is governed by lust, sex, and war—or perhaps, more simply, strife in all matters of life. Indeed, the first act of logos, speech, in *Theogony* is due to hatred and to further the cosmic reality of strife that the poem is saturated in. Gaia speaks to her children after forging a sickle to castrate their hateful and lustful father.

Hesiod composed his epic in a time of cosmological, that is, poetic metaphysical, transformation. It seems to me that Hesiod's composing of the *Theogony* was to challenge the drift of the erotic strife-filled cosmos toward the Homeric cosmos of philia. Consciousness of this older cosmic tradition was threatened, and so Hesiod, as most poets and writers do, recorded for posterity that ancient lore that was being displaced.

Hesiod's poem gruesomely details the birth of the gods: Titans and Olympians, through the violent sexual predation of Uranus upon Gaia. The union of Uranus and Gaia, as Hesiod recounts it, is a cruel and vicious one. Uranus constantly penetrates Gaia at his will and seals their conceived children deep in her womb, which causes her much pain as they grow and move about.

Gaia, in turn—and out of desire for cunning revenge—constructs a sickle and implores one of her children that whoever wields the weapon and overthrows Uranus will have supreme power in the cosmos. Cronus, not so much out of devotion to his mother but hatred of his father, took up the challenge, "Great Uranus came, bringing the night, and spread out around Gaia, desiring philotês, and was extended. His son reached out from ambush with his left hand, and in his right he held the sickle, long and serrated and the genitals of his father he quickly reaped and threw them behind his back to be carried away. But they did not flee from his hand fruitlessly. As many drops of blood spurted forth, all of them Gaia received." The blood from Uranus's castrated phallus fell to the earth giving birth to the furies, monsters, and the other gods, the first being Aphrodite.

Just as the Titans were conceived in violence and ascended through violence, the apple does not fall far from the tree. So, too, the Olympians are conceived in violence and ascend through violence.

Zeus leads the patricidal overthrow of the Titans, just as Cronus had initiated the patricidal usurpation of his father. Hesiod's muses sing of the Titanomachy this way:

"They moved wretched battle, all of them, females and males, on that day, Tritan gods and those who were born from Cronos and those whom Zeus from Erebos beneath the earth brought into light. These were dreadful and strong, possessing excessive force. A hundred arms shot forth from their shoulders, for all of them alike, and each had fifty heads grown out from their shoulders on sturdy limbs. Then, they settled themselves against the Titans in the dire fray, holding huge rocks in their sturdy hands. From the other side, the Titans strengthened their ranks eagerly, and both sides were revealing the works of forceful hands, and the boundless sea resounded dreadfully, and the earth screamed loudly, and wide Uranus groaned when heaved, and from the foundations lofty Olympus shook beneath the fury of the immortals. The heavy pounding of their feet reached murky Tartaros, as did the shrill screams of the terrible pursuit and powerful missiles. Thus they hurled mournful darts at one another. The sound of both reached starry Uranus as they cried out. They clashed with a great war cry."

Clash they did, and the Olympians took their place as heads of the cosmos and the pantheon.

Hesiod's cosmos is a sublimely and spectacularly violent reminder of our primordial sexual and domineering drive. The cosmic reality of the Hesiod's poem is one of divine rape, licentiousness, and male domination and violence. The female gods all suffer at the hand of the more vindictive and lustful male gods. Lastly, the Hesiodic cosmos is truly governed by the *agon*, and that is what the muses sing in celebration of—only the gods with strong wills and the desire for violence are worthy to be sung of.

The Homeric Cosmos

The song of Homer is not the masculine war tale that it initially seems to be. In fact, it is male sexual predation that has caused the Trojan War in the first place. Homer sheds light on the old world of Hesiod that is now being sublated by the cosmos of love. Nevertheless, Homer's cosmos is not an idyllic and fanciful one. It retains all the old seeds of the Hesiodic cosmos but moves beyond it by offering us a path out through the power of love.

The characters that populate Homer's cosmic drama are individuals in oscillation between the two worlds. At one pole are the characters that exude the Hesiodic characteristics of lust, strife, and obscene desire for war. Diomedes is undeniably the most Hesiodic of the Argives. His lustful embrace of conflict leads him to spearing Ares and slashing Aphrodite; not even the sacred is safe from the pillaging spirit of war. Paris is also a character who exudes the erotic impulses of the Hesiodic cosmos. His abduction and rape of Helen is what sparked the war, and he constantly fails in his duties to father and fatherland whenever he sees Helen. The other great character who begins with the Hesiodic spirit—but will overcome it—is Achilles.

The other pole includes the characters that exhibit the new cosmic spirit of love, *philia*, and devotedness—or what the Romans would later call *pietas*, piety. The Trojans tend to be the characters that exercise these virtues like Hector, Aeneas, and Priam. But these virtues are not exclusive to the Trojan heroes. Briseis and Patroclus also serve as calming characters who keep the maelstrom of war from boiling over into complete chaos.

After Agamemnon steals Briseis, causing Achilles to sulk in his tent and refuse to fight, we learn that Briseis was the intended bride to Achilles. Patroclus managed to work out a deal between her and Achilles, which Briseis tearfully reveals when she cries over the body of the dead hero, "But you, Patroclus, you would not let me weep, not when the swift Achilles cut my husband down, not when he plundered the lordly Mynes' city—not even weep! No, again and again you vowed you'd make me godlike Achilles' lawful, wedded wife, you would sail me west in your warships, home to Phthia and there with the Myrmidons hold my marriage feast. So now I mourn your death—I will never stop—you were always kind." Briseis's revelation also reveals something about Patroclus.

Patroclus, that other great hero who has been overshadowed by Achilles, is a kindly man, and he is deeply wise. He is the calming agent in the tent of Achilles. Achilles is only thrown into a rage, that infamous rage the muses sing of, when Patroclus has been slaughtered. It is as if Patroclus serves as the calming barrier preventing the outflowing of Achilles's rage. Patroclus is a character who keeps serenity and conducts order in the strife-filled cosmos. Patroclus is the intermediary conduit of love: the body of love which keeps the rage of Achilles from pouring out in rageful vengeance over the world. The death of Patroclus causes the great unleashing of the rage of Achilles.

With the rage of Achilles now unleashed the world descends into the madness of the Hesiodic cosmos. All order, devotedness, and calm are wiped away in the bloodshed of war. Achilles mercilessly cuts down the Trojans who oppose him. Blood and entrails, once orderly contained in human bodies, spill out chaotically over the sands of Troy. In a very important moment, the royal prince Lycaon throws himself at the madman and weeps for mercy. Achilles lifts up his arm and thrusts his sword into the prince of Troy and vows to wipe out the seed of Priam from the earth. Achilles proceeds to kill Hector and attempts to defile his body by dragging it on the sands and rocks of the beaches of Troy.

Priam, who loves his son, is compelled to venture into the tent of Achilles and convince the killer to return the body of his beloved son. This is a bridge too far. Hector initially attempted to reason with the mad killer before seeing Achilles's hate-filled resolve and losing his nerve before accepting his fate to be slaughtered. We already know that Achilles cannot be reasoned with. Yet Priam's love still pushes him into this tent of despair and danger. And it will not be any rational conversation that leads to the touching conclusion of the *Iliad* but a deep pathological reality, empathy, which brings the epic to its remarkable conclusion.

Inside the tent of Achilles, we witness the metamorphosis of the great Greek killer and the manifestation of the Homeric cosmos. In a recapitulation of images—and understanding the imagery of the *Iliad* is the key to understanding the epic—Priam throws himself at the feet of Achilles, just as Lycaon had done. We have already seen this image before and know what the outcome was. We also know that Achilles has vowed to wipe out Priam's seed from the earth, and he now has the opportunity to do precisely that by killing Priam who defenselessly begs for the return of Hector's body.

Instead of killing Priam, Achilles breaks down and weeps with the King of Troy—the man whom he hates and swore to kill. It is the love a father has for his son (and the memory of a father's love) that breaks Achilles's heart of iron. Love includes relationships and is something that goes beyond the self. Love is that force that binds the world, friends and enemies, together.

The triumph of Homer is in how Achilles finds redemption, salvation, in and through love. And what is more scandalous and shocking than for the greatest killer the world has ever known to be broken down by a weeping and grieving old man who begs defenselessly at his feet before lifting him up and weeping with him in unitive embrace? In the midst of the most famous war in history, it is the feminine that triumphs and brings healing to the world.

Homer's cosmos does not dispense with the lust and strife that defines the Hesiodic cosmos; it still finds itself deeply in bed, pardon the pun, with it. But the grand achievement of Homer is how he turns this cosmos of lust and strife on its head and opens the door to the possibility that this conflictual world can be healed—even if only momentarily—by the power of love. More specifically, the love that helps heal the world is the love parents show their children; for it is the memory of Peleus's love for young Achilles that causes Achilles to empathetically unite with Priam. As Homer powerfully sings, "Overpowered by memory, both men gave way to grief." In that grief, loving empathy overwhelmed Achilles and Priam, and they were united in each other's arms.

The song of Homer is truly powerful because he changes the focus from the gods—though they are ever present—to humans. Homer locates the healing and loving power of the cosmos not in the divines but in human beings. It is humans—not the gods—who bring healing and serenity to a world torn and chaotic. Homer is the first great humanist in the Western tradition and carved out a space for human agency and empathy to triumph over the will and dictates of cruel and petty gods. Empathy that breeds friendship—and forgiveness growing from empathy—is the love that now moves the Homeric cosmos.

Pity and the Euripidean Cosmos

The cosmos of love introduced by Homer undergoes further iterations and developments in Aeschylus and Sophocles. Aeschylus gives us a cosmos of love—love of father and gods—that leads to a new world of persuasion and justice. Sophocles retrenches the importance of the family as the primary nexus where love is fostered and where our redemption is to be found, but he focuses entirely on human devotedness rather than any devotedness to the gods. Euripides chips away at the notion of love and exposes it to be hollow and insufficient; or so Euripides thinks, and so Euripides also transforms the understanding of love from empathy and devotedness to pity.

The war plays of Euripides, of which I would include *Iphigenia in Aulis*, center on women in an admittedly male-dominated world (let us not forget the male-dominated cosmogonic theologies of Hesiod and Homer). Euripides, the foremost ancient deconstructionist until Saint Augustine, tears away the veil of the strife-filled cosmos given a moving makeover by Homer. He returns us to the cruel cosmos of violence, lust, and strife. *Iphigenia in Aulis*, *Hecuba*, the *Trojan Women*, and *Andromache*, all have the haunting images of feminine fertility cruelly expunged by sadistic and toxically masculine men.

Euripides understood that humans learn through images and he also understood the importance placed on the family by his Athenian audience. As such, he scandalously and shockingly strikes at the human heart by depicting the rupture of the family by having children ripped out of the arms, the figurative womb, of the mother by vicious men. (Euripides, therefore, subverts this image of the Hesiodic gods by changing the cruel and vengeful male gods to human males.)

In *Iphigenia in Aulis*, Iphigenia is the only dignified character of the play, wherein she offers herself as the virgin sacrifice to procure the blessings of war. But we should not fall for the romanticism of Iphigenia's self-sacrifice. The play exposes the hollowness and cruelty of sacrifice, Agamemnon, and the Greek lust for violence.

The most touching scene, which is then ruptured in heart-wrenching fashion since we know Iphigenia's fate, is when Iphigenia hugs her mother goodbye in one final embrace. Here, Iphigenia and Clytemnestra are united in love before being torn away by the callous demands of the gods and men's lust for war. We are meant to be moved to pity Iphigenia and her situation and despise Agamemnon for his merciless heart. Pity, Euripides is subtly informing us, is that which will save the world from destruction and disaster.

This emphasis on pity is developed further in the *Trojan Women*, *Hecuba*, and *Andromache*. Euripides describes the Trojan women as pitiable and to be pitied. In the *Trojan Women* and *Hecuba*, Euripides also drives home his stake at children being torn from the arms, womb, of their mothers.

The death of Astyanax is perhaps the most haunting of all the Eurpidean images of a child torn away from their mother. The Greek conquerors of Troy fear that he will grow strong and seek revenge over the death of Hector. Therefore, the Greeks conclude they must kill Astyanax. Astyanax runs to Andromache and embraces his mother in her arms for protection when Talthybius, the reluctant pawn of violence in the play, comes over and tears him away from his mother's arm. Again, this shocking image is meant to evoke the horror of a child being torn away from a mother's womb and elicit strong emotional responses from the audience. The Greek soldiers proceed to throw the young babe head-first down the battlements where he cracks his skull open and dies.

After killing Astyanax, the Greeks return him to the beachhead on their shield. What initially seems to be an image of honor is really a cruel mockery on the part of the Greek soldiers. The young child is curled up as if asleep. The image is meant to convey that tender scene of a loving mother watching over her child. But Andromache is absent. She has been sold off into slavery. It is Hecuba, Astyanax's grandmother, who watches the cruel procession of the mangled body of the baby boy come closer and closer. She weeps, "It is not you but I, your grandmother, an old cityless, childless crone, that has to bury your torn body. Wasted, lost forever, all those cuddles, all that care, all that watching you while you sleep."

This image is recapitulated in the *Trojan Women* when Cassandra is torn apart from the loving embrace of Hecuba and hauled off to slavery with

Agamemnon (where she will die alongside him by the vengeful hand of Clytemnestra in revenge for Iphigenia's sacrificial death). Hecuba painfully laments after this horrifying ordeal, "I saw my virgin daughters, bred for bridegrooms of the highest rank, torn from my arms and all their breeding thrown to foreigners." Throughout the play, Euripides has described Hecuba as the "pitiable woman," but the Greeks show her no pity and often make a mockery of her.

The lack of pity reaches its ugly conclusion in *Hecuba* when the titular former Queen of Troy is transformed from that "most unhappy woman" and "pitiable woman" to a "dog with fire-red eyes." Hecuba has lost everything and has been scorned and shunned by all. In the saddest moment of the play, Polyxena, Hecuba's last daughter, is ripped away from her warm embrace by Odysseus, and she dies at the grave of Achilles. This makes real Polyxena's earlier prophecy of her forthcoming death, "Pitiable woman, you will see me, your pitiable whelp, like a heifer bred in the mountains, torn from your arms and sent down to Hades with my throat cut, to the darkness under the earth, where I, unhappy Polyxena, shall lie among the dead."

What Euripides achieves in this degenerated metamorphosis of Hecuba is how the lack of pity turns us into "dog[s] with fire-red eyes" willing to kill and be cruel to all.

The loss of all her daughters (and the lack of pity displayed by the Greeks) causes Hecuba to plot revenge against Polymestor, a former friend and ally who killed her youngest son, Polydorus, thus depriving Hecuba of all her children. In taking revenge, she blinds Polymestor and has his two sons killed. The cycle of death reaches fruition in Euripides when the woman who was to be pitied is mocked, abused, and beaten down to the point of barbarization.

What Euripides achieves in this degenerated metamorphosis of Hecuba is how the lack of pity turns us into "dog[s] with fire-red eyes" willing to kill and be cruel to all. Love, that "dangerous thing," as Medea says in her eponymous play, is redeemed only by pity according to Euripides. Without pity, love truly is a dangerous thing and the devotedness to fatherland and family often a catalyst for ruin. Thus, we see pity as the highest expression of love in the Euripidean cosmos. We are meant to be shocked by the cruel images in Euripides's play to have compassion and mercy to those cruelly beaten down by cosmic violence. Pity, then, is the great pathological force that heals. The lack of pity, by contrast, causes the world to fall into cruelty, murder, and death.

The Endurance of the Pathological Cosmos

Greek literature does not have a rational or orderly cosmic nature to it until the birth of philosophy, first with Pythagoras and then most famously with Plato. Plato's cosmos is rationally constructed and ordered to purge the dangers of pathos from it. Greek literature, in Plato's estimation, failed in providing the cosmos the necessary ingredients for human life and flourishing. It was irrational and unpragmatic. However, do we need to agree with Plato and embrace the hyper rationalistic and anti-pathological cosmic vision he offered?

The development of Greek literature follows the pattern of pathological progress. We find in Hesiod a pathological cosmos defined by strife and rage, lust and hatred, exhausting itself in war (which is ironic given that our contemporary partisans of love act more akin to the governing spirit of Hesiodic cosmos). We find in Homer, in contradistinction to Hesiod, the birth of love. More specifically, we find love as empathy, which manifests itself in the magnanimous act of forgiveness. This empathetic love in Homer is what heals the war-torn world in a moving and satisfying conclusion, even though we know Achilles is still to be killed and Troy burned. By the time we reach Euripides, we find the cosmic pathos initiated by Hesiod and refined by Homer reaching its acme in pity. Will pity save the world? Many people after Euripides have certainly thought so, Jean-Jacques Rousseau and Adam Smith foremost among the modern philosophers.

Greek literature remains the great wellspring of the human condition because the human condition, defined by pathology moreover than reason, is all wrapped up in the grand epics of Greek poetry and drama. We also find Greek literature to be the battlefield where our great ancestors waged the war for meaning. Those who are adamant that love will trump hate, heal the world, and divinize us are not articulating anything new. The Greeks are still singing to us the songs of humanistic love as the spirit that will heal the world.

This essay was first published by *Merion West*, under the title "Don't Cancel the Classics—We Need Them Now More Than Ever," 12 January 2021.

Chapter 1

On Homer

Homer's *Iliad* is the defining epic of Western literature. Its heroes live on in lore and our collective and individual consciousness. Most of Greek—and Roman literature—is indebted to the epic and its characters. Even modern English literature owes much to Homer's monumental and heroic poem. Indeed, all Western literature owes to the wellspring of Homer. Even literary criticism, if it begins with Alexander Pope, is rooted in Homer's genius and splendor. But what is the moving force of the drama, which sees men and their entrails spilling out, throats slit, as dark crimson blood bathes the sand of Troy?

The *Iliad* begins at the end of the Trojan War with a dispute between Agamemnon, the lord and controller of men, and Achilles, the handsome and long-haired Argive who has fallen in love—so he claims—with Briseis. Agamemnon spurns the priest of Apollo and seizes Briseis for himself. Outraged, Achilles abandons the Greek army and holes himself up in his tent with Patroclus and the rest of the Myrmidons as the beaches and plains of Troy are bathed in the blood and intestines of men of all ages.

*

Homer's epic includes the symbiotic relationship between the heavens and earth, between the gods of Olympus and the men and women of the soil. There are heroes who defy and attack the gods, wounding them and showing the boundless lust unleashed in war. There are heroes who always honor the gods and pour out libations and prayers, thus becoming the instantiated link between heaven and earth. The flesh and blood heroes of the *Iliad* struggle with themselves, their desires, and their psyches. From Helen and Agamemnon, to Paris and Hector, to Achilles and Diomedes, the *dramatis personae* of Homer's poetic rendering of the Trojan War stirs the heart to hatred and sympathy.

As such, Homer's poem includes the vestiges of the old cosmogonic worldview captured by Hesiod. Indeed, the contest between Homer and

Hesiod is a contest between competing cosmogonies. Homer is, in this case, the radical; Hesiod the reactionary. The *Iliad* may have been composed before the *Theogony*, but its message radically differs from that of Hesiod's strife-filled classic. In this regard, and if Giambattista Vico is right about sublime poetry and the strife of the gods being the first instantiation of primitive *logos*, the cosmogony of Hesiod is certainly older than the tragic humanized and humanistic cosmos of Homer.

It is difficult to ascertain any sort of free will in the *Iliad*. It is much easier to see, as Plato implied, that the poetic world was one where humans were the puppets of the gods. Those who live and die, those who gain glory and suffer humiliation, do so only because the gods directly involve themselves in human affairs—deflect arrow and spear shafts into less important characters—or allow the various heroes to have their moment under the sun. Irrespective of this, what is clear is the fatalistic cosmos that Homer occupied and that he was wrestling with in his masterpiece.

Hesiod's *Theogony* is a reminder of the cosmogonic world of the ancient Greeks. Their cosmos teemed with life; the gods were active participants in the world, and heaven and earth were linked together in symbiosis. Hesiod's grand poem details, in brutal fashion, the birth and overthrow of the gods. The Titans and Olympians are the offspring of lustful sex, and as such, they are conceived in hatred for their fathers: Uranus among the Titans and Cronos among the Olympians. The cosmos of Hesiod is filled with strife from start to finish. The muses, who sing the praises to the gods, sing praises only to those who are cunning and power hungry.

The strife of the gods is also an enduring image in Homer. Indeed, it is central to it. There is not a moment of peace between the gods. Zeus is repeatedly enraged at Hera and Athena. Athena and Hera conspire against Aphrodite. A wounded Ares is scolded by an angered Zeus. Poseidon holds Zeus in contempt for usurping the position of lord among the gods when the world was agreed to be split in thirds between Zeus, Poseidon, and Hades. Hera seduces Zeus, which causes chaos to spill out over the fields of Troy. In this respect, Homer's depiction of heavenly Olympus is not far removed from Hesiod's brutal and bleak depiction of patricide and usurpation.

As a matter of fact, Homer's Olympus is much like Pseudo-Apollodorus's Olympus. In the *Bibliotheca*, Pseudo-Apollodorus compiles the arc of Greek mythology—thus preserving the wellspring of ancient Greek consciousness. The narrative mythology behind Troy's doom begins in an event reminiscent of the first image of Achilles's god-made shield: a wedding banquet. But mere mortals are not the main guests of honor. The main guests of honor are the gods. All but the goddess of strife, Eris.

There is irony in the goddess of strife not receiving an invitation to the wedding of Peleus and Thetis. If Hesiod's account of the birth of the gods is just the capturing of the most ancient and sublime myth of cosmogonic strife and violence, then all the gods present at the wedding feast of Peleus and Thetis have the energy of strife running through them. Eris, however, is wroth at her exclusion. She tosses the apple of discord in the midst of Aphrodite, Athena, and Hera. The three goddesses quarrel with each other over who is the most beautiful and approach Zeus to settle the dispute.

Zeus, we are told, abdicates his providential responsibility. Instead, he shifts the burden of responsibility to the lustful shepherd Paris. According to Pseudo-Apollodorus's story, Zeus abdicates for two reasons. First, he doesn't want to be the target of the enmity of the two goddesses he does not choose as the most beautiful. Second, by allowing Paris to choose he has a *casus belli* to destroy Troy (because of overpopulation).

The wedding of Peleus and Thetis is much like the image of the wedding banquet and the peaceful city forged on the Shield of Achilles. The supposedly peaceful image is filled with strife. The apple doesn't fall far from the tree in this regard.

Homer's cosmos was a fatalistic one. It was bleak, dark, and filled with strife—that enduring image that carries the *Iliad* forward to its sudden and remarkable conclusion with Priam in the tent of Achilles.

But Homer's sacrilegious, perhaps even impious, inversion of the strife-filled cosmos through the human characters that move the reader's heart to fury and sympathy is part of his triumph as poet and thinker. The gods may be present, but the real action, the real learning, the real progress, is made among the fated heroes of the epic. Homer turns the strife-filled cosmogonic portrait of 8th-century Greece on its head. In doing so, he crafts the greatest love epic in the history of Western literature until Dante's *Divine Comedy*.

Homer shows the gods in their naked vanity. Where Hesiod's muses sing of gods, titans, and monsters, Homer's muses sing of a man—Achilles. This subtle shift is important. The focus of the *Iliad* is not the gods but mortals. Specifically, it is the song of tragic Achilles in faraway Ilium. We are told of the rage of Achilles, but Achilles's rage subsides to love by the end of his story arc.

*

This returns us to where the epic begins, in the final days of Troy and a dispute between Agamemnon and Achilles. Agamemnon is the lord of men and a king who has nothing but the lust for power and glory moving through his fibers. The lust for glory, the lust for power, had so consumed Agamemnon that Aeschylus reminds us that this is what moves Agamemnon—indeed, his entire house, including Clytemnestra, in his play about the King of Mycenae. The chorus, after Cassandra has finished personifying the oracle of reckoning and death, breaks out in collective chant: "But the lust for power never dies—men cannot have enough." Conveniently, the chorus chants this collective wisdom just as Agamemnon is murdered behind the scenes.

In the mad lust of Agamemnon, he spurns the priest of Apollo which enrages the god of the sun, and he also steals Briseis from Achilles's tender and loving arms (or so Achilles claims). Truly, as Aeschylus said, "the lust for power never dies—men cannot have enough." And Agamemnon cannot have enough. But Agamemnon's lusts, his immoral and impious actions—from sacrificing his daughter, Iphigenia, to stealing Briseis, to spurning the priest of Apollo—cause him nightmares and a guilty conscience throughout the epic.

The second great image on the Shield of Achilles is the city at war. Strife dominates the background of that image but the multitude of figures in that image, men and women, young and old, soldiers and non-combatants, are all focused in this hour of strife. It is as if strife also allows for the opportunity to control the passions that times of peace allow to run unbounded, unimpeded, unrestrained. In strife one can harness the power of his devotion, of his love, and focus it to something specific—even if it be life or death in war in the service of the gods, family, and country.

Homer's genius is that the first image is the mythic image of the gods in the heavens that all of listeners would have known. As mentioned, it harkens back to the wedding of Peleus and Thetis and the strife involved in that wedding banquet. The cosmos of strife harkens back to the collective consciousness of the agonistic cosmos that Hesiod put to paper in *Theogony*. The second image embodies the lived reality of Homer's epic as it unfolds. The *Iliad* is a story of strife found in war:

> Strife and Havoc plunged in the fight, and violent Death—now seizing a
> man alive with fresh wounds, now one unhurt, now hauling a dead man

through the slaughter by the heels, the cloak on her back stained red with human blood.

Both images permeate the Greek cosmos and understanding of life just as much as both images pay homage and subvert that collective consciousness of the Greek past.

The *Iliad* is not a story about the gods. It is a story about men and women. It is a story of contrasts. Of growth and humiliation. Of lust and love. Of despair and triumph. The human characters of Homer's grand epic embody what Homer is driving home at with his poem: the tension between strife and love, or lust and love.

The city at war, most immediate of which is Troy, but which also encompasses all the cities involved in the war, focuses on a very specific goal. The enjoyment of peace, of the love afforded in peace, is impossible. The enjoyment of war, the lust unleashed in war, rampages through the pages of the *Iliad* like a tsunami.

Our Homeric heroes embody this epic strife between lust and love that, according to Homer, moves the cosmos instead of only strife. Among those characters who embody lust are Diomedes, Agamemnon, and Paris. Diomedes's lust is so pernicious and wild-flowing that he even wounds Aphrodite and spears Ares in his rage. Not even the sacred can escape the punishing power of lust. Moreover, Diomedes's strife and rage is manifested during the funeral games for Patroclus. Agamemnon is so consumed by the lust for strife that he is deceived by Zeus in a dream and launches a futile attack soon after stealing Briseis from Achilles's arms. He is obstinate throughout the poem and doesn't want to apologize for his actions because of his self-conceited ego. Paris would prefer to soothe his sexual appetites rather than fight Menelaus with honor. "Come—let's go to bed, let's lose ourselves in love," Paris tells Helen after being wounded and whisked away by Aphrodite.

Helen embodied lust in her life before reaching the shores of Troy. In the story she struggles to come to terms with her lustful desires and her strife-filled past. In the presence of Hector she acknowledges that strife governs, or governed, her life. "Bitch that I am" and "Whore that I am" are uttered from her lips to Hector. Helen veers between the poles of strife and orderly love behind the ordered walls and life offered in Troy. She laments that her free-wheeling life of lustful strife has come to an end.

In lamenting this movement away from strife, she comes to embody the possibility of what a life of love can consummate. It is unsurprising that she speaks to Hector of this metamorphosis occurring despite the repercussions of her actions to herself and much of the world. Furthermore, when Hector's body is returned to Troy, she flings herself onto his body and laments his death—recalling how Hector always showed her nothing but love and calmed storms of rage against her with reasoned words of persuasion.

Hector is the character who best embodies ordered love in the poem. His very name, in Greek, means "one who holds together." Hector holds together the worlds of strife and love within him. Hector is also the man blessed with a family in the midst of strife, and his family is a peaceful pole in the turbulence of war. Andromache and Astyanax exude a calming force over Hector, even Astyanax's uncontrollable weeping brings out the intimacy of Hector's caressing and tender love as he strips off his armor and holds his infant son in his arms.

Piety is the great virtue of Hector. When Helenus tells him to return to Troy and offer up libations at Athena's shrine, Hector complies: "So [Helenus] urged and Hector obeyed his brother start to finish." When Hector reaches the gates of Troy he implores the women to fulfill their sacred duties too. "Pray to the gods" are his first words upon returning to his city. Hector's patriotic heart "races to help [his] Trojans" throughout the poem. Hector is a man of family, faith, and fatherland. It is true that "man-killing Hector" is unhinged right before his death, but the shifting—or breaking—of Hector from the man who holds the worlds of mortal love and immortal strife together causes the great resolution of Homer's epic: Hector's death at the hand of Achilles and Priam's retrieval of Hector's body from Achilles's blood-stained fingers.

Patroclus and Briseis give order to each other, or at least Patroclus brought order to Briseis. Patroclus curbed the rage of Achilles as well—until his death at Hector's hands. The internal rage of Achilles never floods outward thanks to Patroclus's calming presence in his tent. When Briseis sees the dead body of Patroclus, she weeps over him like Achilles and the other Greek heroes. In her darkest hours it was Patroclus's kindness that kept her ordered and free from being consumed by the strife of grief.

> But you, Patroclus, you would not let me weep, not when the swift Achilles cut my husband down, not when he plundered the lordly Mynes' city—not even weep! No, again and again you vowed you'd make me godlike Achilles' lawful, wedded wife, you would sail me west in your

warships, home to Phthia and there with the Myrmidons hold my marriage feast. So now I mourn your death—I will never stop—you were always kind.

Briseis is another character who brings love and order out of the heroes of the poem. As mentioned, Patroclus apparently treats her with abundant kindness after her city is sacked by the Greeks and her family killed by Achilles. She is the loved person of Achilles, the bride or bride-to-be of the rage-filled son of Peleus and Thetis. Even when hauled off by Agamemnon, the lord and controller of men claims he never slept with her. For whatever reason, Briseis is a sacred subject whom even lustful Agamemnon doesn't violate.

Achilles, however, is a character in oscillation between the two poles much like Helen. Achilles loved Briseis, at least if we can trust Achilles. When Diomedes and Odysseus rendezvous with Achilles, carrying Agamemnon's offer to bring Achilles back into the fight, the wounds of Achilles run very deep in his soul. He is the lover spurned and, as such, is filled with internal strife and hatred. He rages with the same rage that he had unleashed in the previous ten years of war which earned him immortal fame and glory. But in rebuking Agamemnon, Achilles makes clear, "he keeps the bride I love" (referring to Briseis). Achilles professes his love for Briseis and considers her his bride. A man can only love once, "but a man's life breath cannot come back again—no raiders in force, no trading brings it back, once it slips through a man's clenched teeth."

The love that Achilles has for Briseis is no love at all. It is self-centered, self-focused. It is a love that cannot lead to relationships. It is a love that is, in fact, a form of lust.

Achilles must learn to overcome this self-centered lust, which he conveniently veils with the language of love to distract him from this important awakening. Love requires people. Love moves beyond the self to others. So self-absorbed is Achilles, he lets thousands of lovers perish and thousands of families fall ruined forever. That is the price of strife as Homer so poignantly captures when he brutally details the gore and violence of men's limbs being hacked off, throats slashed, and blood gushing onto the sandy plains of Troy of men no longer able to make love to their wives, brides, or enjoy the company of parents and children ever again.

Chaos and strife demand the ordered internal organs of man to spill out on the battlefield. As the scheming of the gods reaches its peak with the death of Patroclus and Hector's transformation from orderly lover to rampaging killer, it takes Achilles, donned with his new shield, to confront the storm of Hector. So Achilles does. He ventures forth to avenge the death of his beloved friend whom the Greeks defended and returned to his tent in one of the most chilling and stirring episodes of the entire poem.

But Achilles's killing of Hector does not end the story. Achilles reverts to the mad dog he is by dragging and attempting to defile the body of Hector through the dust and rocks of the earth. The gods, however, preserve Hector's body from such animalistic defilement. Timocratic society knows only of glory, of honor, of ambition—in other words, the glorification of heroic strife.

This bleak portrait of a world governed by strife is precisely what Homer is slowly subverting by the resolution of the *Iliad* (and fully revealed by the conclusion of the *Odyssey* with the safe return of Odysseus to Penelope and Telemachus).

*

According to Plato, part of the reality of love is the reality of loss or separation. When Aristophanes's grand myth of love is presented in the *Symposium*, Plato's use of comic equivalence is meant to convey that Aristophanes's account of love is partially accurate. Aristophanes is meant to look like a mad and raving fool, but he is right that love does entail some form of loss or yearning for a missing half. In losing Briseis and Patroclus, Achilles's love turned to lustful rage, but in that rage the tiny seed of love is revealed.

When Priam enters Achilles's tent to implore the return of Hector's body, this most moving scene—which concludes Homer's epic—is the triumph of Homer and the redemption of Achilles. In the *Odyssey*, Achilles informs Odysseus that he'd rather be alive as a poor farmer with his family rather than be the master over the dead: "I'd rather slave on earth for another man—some dirt-poor tenant farmer who scrapes to keep alive—than rule down here over all the breathless dead. But come, tell me the news about my gallant son." Achilles learned this value of love and family in the presence of Priam. In handing Hector's body back to a loving father, Achilles comes to understand that love includes more than the self.

Love includes relationships. Love involves others. Love is the bond that brings even enemies together in healing. Love transcends all boundaries. Achilles and Priam weep together in each other's arms because it is the love of a father, and the memory of a father's love, which breaks the ironed heart of Achilles to be a vessel of love and intimacy again.

Homer's *Iliad* concludes without the end of the war. Troy is still to be sacked. Achilles is still to be killed. But the conclusion of the *Iliad* is fitting and fulfilling because the arc of coming to know and exude love is what the poem is about—long and excruciating as this process is. It is the story of Achilles's transformation from rage-filled and strife-filled killer to forgiving lover touched by the very power of love. That is why the conclusion of the *Iliad* is so inspiring, so moving, so touching, indeed, so enduring after nearly three millennia.

Achilles has come to learn—as revealed at the end of the *Iliad* and stated by his own tongue in the *Odyssey*—that love is what brings order to strife. Or perhaps truer to the ancient psyche, love is what orders the reality of strife to something good and beautiful: the beauty and the good of the family. It is a father's love for his son that causes Achilles to understand the magnanimity of love and the forgiveness that accompanies love.

In his rage Achilles brutally slaughters the sons of Priam before attempting to desecrate the body of Hector in his blood-thirsty rage. Achilles wants to wipe the world clean of the seed of Priam out of his hatred for Priam, Hector, and the rest of the Trojans. This is what makes the conclusion of the *Iliad* so powerful and moving. We have just seen Achilles spill out the bowels of Priam's sons begging for their life and spear and drag Hector's body as the ultimate sign of defilement. Achilles's strife-filled rage, however, is transformed into a forgiving and healing love in the arms of Priam. Priam throws himself at the knees and feet of Achilles, just as Lycaon had done in begging for his life. The previous image of Achilles in this domineering position was one in which he brutally killed a royal son of Troy. But in the concluding image, Achilles embraces Priam in love rather than spilling out his entrails over the ground and on his feet in a fit of rage and domineering lust.

The triumph of Homer is magnificent and enduring. He turns the cosmos of strife on its head and places the centrality of love in this chaotic cosmos in the hearts of human beings. If Hector held the balance between strife and love together in his life before becoming unhinged by Zeus's diabolical scheming, it was Achilles's act of love to Priam that brought healing to the broken world around Troy in his return of Hector's body to his loving father. The torch was passed from Hector to Achilles and the redemption of Achilles is completed in his act of magnanimity to Priam. After Achilles's death that torch is passed on to Odysseus whose love for Penelope and Telemachus drives him across the turbulent seas and to escape the lusts of Circe and Calypso to reunite with his wife and son and enjoy that orderly feast denied to Peleus and Thetis, denied to the women and men in the peaceful city on Achilles's shield, and denied to all the breathless dead slaughtered in war (more on this in a moment).

The *Iliad* is a grand love poem on a cosmic scale. This epic of love moves heaven and earth. It is a poem that wrestles with the agonism between love and strife. It is a poem that moves beyond the strife-filled cosmos of Hesiod and Homer's predecessors. It is the poem that brings love into the cosmos and gives us the faintest glimpse of hope that love can move heaven and earth and bring the joyful rest that the strife-filled human heart seeks. Lastly, the love that Homer inserts into the cosmos is a love that heals and forgives. That is why the *Iliad* is an eternal work and deserving to be read as a classic par excellence; for in Homer's great song the birth of a cosmos of love through forgiveness is brought forth amid the dark ruins of capricious gods and human lust leading to death and destruction. An act of heroic forgiveness brings peace to the world. We mustn't forget that Homer ends his grand epic on the peace bestowed to Priam by Achilles.

*

Homer, as we can tell, was a poet with an agenda. While it is fashionable to sideswipe Homer as having never existed, serious classicists, like M.L. West, know that Homer—"the poet"—was real. A careful study of Homer's language and epic composition certainly suggests that a final redactor stood over the finished product of the *Iliad* with a significant contribution to its final form and message. The verdict is outstanding on the Homer of the *Odyssey*, to which I agree with classicists like West that the poet of the *Odyssey* is not the same as the poet of the *Iliad*, but pedantic concerns of authorship distract us from the content and message of the *Odyssey* and the fact that final redactor also stood over the final composition of that great work which bears Homer's name. We should address the content of the *Odyssey* rather than the endless question of Homeric authorship which bores people away from its remarkable content; when we do, the Homer of the *Odyssey* was also a poet with an agenda.

It is deeply lamentable that in our iconoclastic age Homer is being pillaged by our supposed guardians of culture. W.H. Auden must be weeping in his grave. It is commonplace to hear how Homer glorified violence, "toxic" male masculinity, and represents the fountainhead of everything to be despised in today's humanities department: the dead white European male. Such views do a great injustice to Homer, for Homer soars above all later literati because of his upending the Hesiodic masculine fantasy and giving to posterity the quintessential heroic ideal of love embracing death that has moved all subsequent great art and stories. The Homeric revolution was, first and foremost, a call to the power of love: Achilles and Patroclus, Hector and Andromache, Priam and Hector, Achilles and Priam, and, of course, the most famous of all: Odysseus and Penelope.

The Homer, of the *Iliad*, as I've written elsewhere, is the first humanist in the West and advanced a song of love and forgiveness.[*] The Homer of the *Odyssey*, as we know, articulates the song of the returning husband and the restoration of the family. Taken in continuity, the Trojan War begins in marital infidelity and is only ended through marital fidelity. Quite the odyssey, all things considered. The humanism of the *Iliad* is retained in the humanism of the *Odyssey*; our epics sing of mortal men and the deeply flawed passions rather than the gods and immortality (as Hesiod does in the *Theogony*). The torch of human love is passed from Hector, Priam, and Achilles to Odysseus, Telemachus, and Penelope in this continuity of heroic humanisms in the Homeric epics.

Competing Heroisms

Homer was concerned with composing an epic that subtly challenged the violent heroism praised by Hesiod. As I've previously stated, "*The Iliad* is not an epic of hyper masculinity and war as it can easily and superficially appear to be at first glance. Rather, it is a grand love poem of cosmic scope and proportions. For the *Iliad* is not merely a love story like a romance between two individuals but a love story that brings forth salvation in the cold and dark cosmos governed by lustful strife, war, and rape." The heroic ideal in the *Iliad*, exemplified by Hector, Patroclus, and Achilles, stand in stark contrast to their heroic foils who stand with their feet firmly planted in the Hesiodic cosmos: Diomedes, Menelaus, and Agamemnon. Homer's *Iliad* presents a subtle

---

[*] See my essay "Reading Homer From Here to Eternity," *VoegelinView*, June 1, 2020. It is also included in my book *The Odyssey of Love: A Christian Guide to the Great Books* (Eugene OR: *Wipf and Stock*, 2021).

critique of martial greatness in contrast to loving kindness—the highest heroism of all.

The heroism of Hector is not in his martial prowess (though he certainly has that) but his soft, caressing, tenderness on the walls of Troy as he strips off his war armor to hold his weeping son Astyanax and comfort his distraught wife, Andromache. Likewise, the heroism of Patroclus is the healing touch he provides to Eurypylus as he staggers back to the Achaean ships with an arrow wound in his thigh and the other Greeks who remember his loving kindness after his death including Menelaus and Briseis. The heroism of Achilles reaches its magnanimous manifestation in his forgiving Priam and lifting him up as a friend, bestowing peace, and returning Hector's body rather than his battlefield fury.

If Homer articulated an alternative vision of heroism contra Hesiod, what was the Hesiodic ideal of heroism? Let's briefly remind ourselves.

Hesiod's *Theogony*, as hitherto stated, gives us the portrait of the poet's sublime imagination, a heroism rooted in sexual violence, lust, and castration; of conflict, war, and usurpation. The muses sing of Zeus, the one god among many gods and ancient deities who ascended to the top of Olympus through unmitigated violence. Violence, as any reader of Hesiod's sublime poem knows, is what is celebrated. There is the sexual violence of Uranus over Gaia; the patricidal violence of Kronos as he castrates Uranus; and the usurping violence of Zeus who leads the Olympians in overthrowing the Titans. Zeus then slays Typhoeus and cements his headship over the pantheon.

From the pen and mind of Hesiod, violence is the heroic ideal. In Homer, violence is deconstructed—as Caroline Alexander wrote in her wonderful work *The War That Killed Achilles*—and turned on its head. The Hesiodic ideal of heroism is found wanting from Homer's magisterial mind. Homeric heroism is found in the magnanimity of healing love; forgiveness is the highest manifestation of that heroism. At least in the *Iliad*.

The heroic ideal of Homer in the *Odyssey* is different from the magnanimous forgiveness articulated in the *Iliad* (as just covered). The heroism of the *Iliad* has a cosmopolitan intent to it: forgiveness of an enemy. The heroism of the *Odyssey* has a traditional imperative to it: restoration of the family. But that is too superficial of a reading, however true the basic thesis is. The heroic ideal of the *Odyssey* goes far beyond the mere returning husband and filial restoration and is also equally as deep as the magnanimous heroism articulated in the *Iliad* as we journey into the underworld of metaphysics and human nature for the first time through the song of the "man of twists and turns."

The Heroic Imagination of the *Odyssey*

The song of a returning husband only glances the surface of the monumental, though flawed, achievement of the heroic ideal in the *Odyssey*. Love and its relationship to death is one of the seminal topics of philosophical inquiry. It has captured the imagination of writers from Greek antiquity, the biblical authors, Richard Wagner, to my former teacher Sir Roger Scruton. The Homer of the *Odyssey* offers his genius to the competing images of heroism: to embrace death through love (the love of a mortal no less who shares in our mortal love). In the unescapable reality of mortality, that common condition we all share, we find the highest manifestation of heroism—the acceptance of death and our refusal to run from it.

"Sing to me of the man, Muse, the man of twists and turns driven time and again off course, once he had plundered the hallowed heights of Troy." The opening of the *Odyssey*, like the *Iliad*, is deeply radical when compared against Hesiod. Hesiod's muses sing of gods: "From the Muses of Helicon let us bring our singing, that haunt Helicon's great and holy mountain, and dance on their soft feet round the violet-dark spring and the altar of the mighty son of Kronos . . . From there they go forth, veiled in thick mist, and walk by night, uttering beautiful voice, singing of Zeus who bears the aegis." Homer's muses sing of mortal men. The conscionable shift is from the heavens (Hesiod) to the earth (Homer) and makes the realm of mortality the principal focus of action. Homer, right from the start, informs us that his heroism is about us: flesh and blood human beings and not the immortal gods and nymphs who often wreak havoc over the world and their human playthings.

The Odyssey begins with a family estranged; Telemachus, the son of Odysseus, is despondent about the declination of his household. Many suitors have occupied the home of Odysseus and begun courting, or trying to seduce, Penelope. Telemachus doesn't get on well with any of the suitors, especially Antinous—the most vile and violent of the suitors. That the *Odyssey* begins with Telemachus and his journeys to find his father is important. The epic is larger than just Odysseus though the epic bears his name. While the Odyssey is named after Odysseus, it includes the trials and journeys of Telemachus and Penelope. It encompasses a world of many people. It is an epic of the family rather than a single individual even if a single individual is the primary protagonist.

But after Telemachus sets sail to find his father, the perspective shifts to Odysseus and the song becomes the story we all know. The great warrior and strategist, schemer and trickster, is now shipwrecked on Calypso's Island. Calypso has held Odysseus captive for seven years, fallen madly in love with him, and still wants to keep the king of Ithaca as her sexual captive.

Odysseus has two encounters with femme fatale divinities in the epic: Calypso and Circe. While ideologically driven feminist readings want to cast Calypso and Circe in the victimized position resonate with the twenty-first century's political *zeitgeist*, the reality is that Odysseus has been victimized by Calypso and Circe. Moreover, it is critical that we understand Odysseus's refusal to transcend his mortality for their immortality. For that is what they offer to him: immortality and unlimited sexuality, the two things that male nature supposedly seeks and which Odysseus himself is often guilty of exhibiting. Odysseus has before him the fantastical dream of every man: immortality and sex. He ultimately gives that up for mortality with his family.

It is also fashionable, considering the exoteric narrative, to condemn Odysseus for his infidelity to Penelope. Penelope, who has wasted away the prime of her life with her husband gone, remains faithful to Odysseus throughout the narrative. Yet so too does Odysseus's yearning heart seek restoration with Penelope. Odysseus, as Eva Brann noted in her work *Homeric Moments*, does overcome the temptations of Calypso and Circe. He remains a dutiful husband, brushing away transcendent transfiguration for the fleeting nature of mortality. But why?

The Odyssey is a story about a story. It is a song of heroic pilgrimage. Once we recognize that Odysseus shuns immortality and embraces the decaying reality of Ithaca, of Penelope and Telemachus, we realize that it is a journey to death accompanied by love that makes death worthwhile; for the love that Odysseus embodies is the love that makes death painless. It is the love that brings serenity amid chaos, darkness, and death.

Now we begin to see that the *Odyssey* is more than a song about finding a home, returning to a home, or the homestead—as is fashionable from conservative readings of the epic. The real heroism sung of in the *Odyssey* is the acceptance of mortality (our human nature), the embrace of love and in that embrace of love the acceptance of death (the fullest reality of human nature). Odysseus can be a sexual captive, a sexual slave, to the goddesses; he spurns this sexual immortality for the fleeting heartbeats of Penelope and Telemachus. The heroism that is extolled in the *Odyssey* is the heroism that embraces mortal nature against the phantasmagoria of transcendence, a heroism that embraces the imperfect beauty of this world rather than the illusory beauty of the divines.

When Odysseus makes landfall and is taken to the Phaeacians he recounts his adventure to the intrigued court. Odysseus, as we know from the *Iliad*, was one of the heroes of the Trojan War. He played a prominent role in the destruction of Troy. Yet that is not what Odysseus tells his Phaeacian hosts (or at least, this is not what Homer wants to retell within the *Odyssey*). Instead, he recounts that odyssey of "twists and turns" that has led him to their island. He sings of the trials and tribulations of his return turned tragic sojourn. The song that we ought to remember about Odysseus is his journey toward that mortal love which calls him home, not his military exploits.

If the Homer of the *Odyssey* wanted to praise martial virtue like Hesiod, he had every opportunity to do so. Instead, our poet sings of the heroism of the binding reality of love; a love that sees Telemachus search for his father, Penelope remains true to her wedding vows despite all the pressures thrust onto her by the suitors, and Odysseus forsake the offer of immortal transcendence and eternal pleasure for mortal decay and fleeting peace. It is far more heroic, Homer is asserting through the epic, to embrace the realities of mortal love than masculine gory-glory or eternal sexual pleasure with the gods.

The song of heroic mortality and filial love reaches its climax in the underworld. Odysseus journeys into the realm of the dead and meets the heroes of the Trojan Wars and the temptations of sexual desire. There, Odysseus meets Agamemnon, Ajax, and Achilles; he also sees many of the most beautiful women in Greek lore: Antiope, Alcmena, Megara, Epicaste, and Chloris.

Conversing with Agamemnon about his demise, the King of the Myceneans exclaims, "Odysseus, mastermind of war, I was not wrecked in the ships when lord Poseidon roused some punishing blast of stormwinds, gust on gust, nor did ranks of enemies mow me down on land—Aegisthus hatched my doom and my destruction, he killed me, he with my own accursed wife." Agamemnon warns against a woman's trust. Implicitly, he is suggesting that Odysseus shouldn't be so foolish as to seek a running return with his wife; though Agamemnon qualifies this implicit rebuke by suggesting that Penelope won't betray him as Clytemnestra betrayed Agamemnon.

Talking to Achilles, the reality of the embrace of love and death under the bond of the family is brought to the fore. Odysseus showers Achilles—that terror of the Trojans—with praise. Achilles rebuffs the praise Odysseus gives him. Achilles says the most memorable lines of the poem, "I'd rather slave on earth for another man—some dirt-poor tenant farmer who scrapes to keep alive—than rule down here over all the breathless dead. But come, tell me the news about my gallant son."

Achilles, far from having satisfaction in ruling "over all the breathless dead," is a grieving a wounded soul because he had abandoned his family and now seeks to hear the news of his gallant son Neoptolemus. Odysseus obliges and tells the great killer what he knows. But what Achilles desires—too late for him, however—is not immortal fame but mortal love. Achilles would have rather spent an unfamous life as "some dirt-poor tenant farmer" so long as he cradled his children and caressed his wife as he tells Odysseus. But the vainglory of war tempted him; all for naught. Achilles, here, serves as a warning in the Odyssey.

The revelations that come in the middle of the book, in the realm of the dead, have something in common: filial betrayal. Agamemnon was betrayed by his wife. Achilles is distraught for having abandoned his family. Both implore Odysseus not to make the same mistake.

Embracing Love and Death

As Odysseus finishes his story to the Phaeacians he embarks to sail the final waves to Ithaca. Athena, as we know, continues to aid her favorite son. Ithaca is revealed. Odysseus reunites with Telemachus. The man of "twists and turns" learns of what has befallen his kingdom and the scheming plots hatched by the many suitors. Despite the messy world of mortal love and lust, betrayal and deceit, Odysseus still opts to choose mortality with Penelope and Telemachus instead of immortality (and eternal pleasure) with Calypso or Circe.

As in the *Iliad*, the *Odyssey* is radical in its humanistic disposition. The gods factor prominently just like before, but the gods are neither the subjects of praise (as in Hesiod) nor the subjects of our salvation. Instead, what is praised is the choice of a man—guided by Athena, the virgin goddess of wisdom, to be sure—to choose love and death with his family rather than eternal and immortal bliss with the fleeting shadows of the divines. After all, that is how the poem ends. Odysseus reclaims his home by vanquishing the suitors. Athena comes to restore peace at the poem's conclusion. Odysseus is reunited with his family and the long arduous Trojan War and all its associated labors and pains have come to an end.

Though the poem ends on this note of peace, the implied ending is far more dramatic than the peace orchestrated by reason (Athena). Odysseus, as we know, is mortal. As are Penelope and Telemachus. The immortal fame of Odysseus is not in his martial exploits but his forsaking transcendence for mortality; the hero's embrace of his mortal nature is the highest manifestation of the heroic spirit to Homer and that's what he wanted us to remember through the *Odyssey*. And what guides this embrace of mortality? Love. Odysseus would rather die, in love, than live in servitude and a slave to passions. And rather than sing about the Odysseus who was a great warrior, Homer sings to us that song of Odysseus choosing to die, in love, rather than live forever in servitude and a slave to his passions.

Mortality makes love meaningful because it creates an imperative for love whereas the immortality of love offered by the divines leads to enslavement, an end to that imperative offered through our mortality. It is precisely this dichotomy that Homer brings to the fore in Odysseus's "twists and turns" as he navigates the empty world of loveless immortality—whatever its comforts—back to the world of loving mortality despite its hardships and inevitability of death. The love offered by Calypso and Circe is no love at all. Their divinity is their unreality. Only the mortal flesh of another human heart can satiate Odysseus's yearning heart.

The universality of the *Odyssey* is not in its political message but in its metaphysical message. And this is why Homer is now scorned; we live in a world that shuns metaphysics for the pure ideologies of the political *zeitgeist*. But Homer stands as an enduring challenge to that farce. The political heroes are all dead: Agamemnon, Ajax, Achilles, Aegisthus, Clytemnestra. Political entities rise and fall: Troy is destroyed, Mycenae in ruins, and Ithaca—in Homer's time—is far from the fabled kingdom associated with Odysseus.

Mortal love, a love between humans in contrast to political glory, is what is heroically sung about in the epic of twists and turns; twists and turns of the heart, but twists and turns that lead us to embrace who we are: mortal lovers fated to die in each other's arms but in the tender caressing hold of a lover all the worries of the world dissipate in that blissful serenity offered in love. That is the most heroic ideal we can live, and it is open to everyone: from dirt-poor tenant farmers to kings and queens and everyone else in between. The Homer of the *Odyssey* gives us the first great epic that calls us to embrace mortal love as our greatest calling.

The *Odyssey* portrays for us the universal twists and turn of the human heart common to all—its desire for transcendence but the renunciation of that illusory phantasmagoria for the warm reality of a human embrace, an embrace that inevitably leads to our death, but a death that is more heroic than anything achieved by those who burned Troy. Homer calls us home. That home is more than a piece of land. More than a title of kingship. It is where the heart finds its embrace of the mortal other, destined to decay and die, but decay and die together in a loving embrace of serenity as we watch the sun set for the final time. There is nothing more heroic than that. And it is fitting that the Homeric journey which began in marital infidelity comes to a heroic conclusion in marital fidelity; where lust led to war in the beginning, love leads to peace at the end. Love is the only way home. Love is the only reality that brings peace.[*]

This chapter is adapted from two essays: "Homer's Iliad and the Shield of Love and Strife" first published by *The Imaginative Conservative*, 8 August 2019 and "The Real Heroism of Odysseus" published by *Merion West*, 10 December 2021.

---

[*] The post-Homeric, or extra-Homeric, material is not a concern for us when reading Homer. As it relates to Odysseus, the now lost *Telegony*, details the death of Odysseus at the hands of a son borne by Circe, Telegonus. The straightforward message is Fate is cruel and you cannot escape it (it is prophesied that Odysseus would die by his son). Telegonus, however, returns to Aeaea with Odysseus's dead body, buries him, and marries Penelope. Telemachus marries Circe. In a roundabout way, though, the *Telegony* also tells the story of how love in marriage brings peace, even immortality, for Penelope and Telemachus are made immortal in their marriages are their grief over Odysseus's death is assuaged in their new marriages. Nevertheless, the Homer of the *Odyssey* gives us a powerful story of love in mortality, embracing human love rather than the false love offered by the gods. *The Telegony*, as an epic, was believed to have existed around 700 B.C.. The poet of the *Odyssey*, whom we call Homer, would have been familiar with it. Yet he decided not to include its material in his work. The extra-Homeric (or post-Homeric) literature is wonderful in its own and deserves to be dealt with on their own accord. Taken in combination with Homer, we see the broader human wrestling with their stories and meanings. For us, however, in this chapter only Homer's message concerns us—for when reading Homer what Homer provided is what we wrestle with.

Chapter 2

Why *The Oresteia* Still Matters

It is said that the *Oresteia* is the ancient world's *Divine Comedy*, with some justification. Originally a four-part play, only three pieces of the movement survive: *Agamemnon*, the *Libation Bearers*, and the *Eumenides*. The finale, *Proteus*, was a cosmic dance of the gods and heroes, the full fruition of the work's manifestation—the waltz of the heavens and earth in harmony already implied and presupposed at the conclusion of the *Eumenides*. From the murder of Agamemnon to the revenge taken by Orestes, his flight to Athens, and exoneration before the court of Apollo and Athena, the *Oresteia* moves from "hell" to "purgatory" to "paradise." Yet the *Oresteia*, written two and a half millennia ago, touches on themes still so relevant today: justice, injustice, revenge, and gender conflict. Its themes touch on the eternal relevance of the human condition and struggle with much consideration for how to live today.

Aeschylus lived through the golden age of Greece and Athens. In his thirties, he was a hoplite in the army that defeated the Persians at Marathon. Living through the Second Persian Wars, he experienced the tumultuous sack and burning of Athens by Persian forces after the Hellenic allies led by Sparta were defeated at Thermopylae. Aeschylus subsequently fought with the victorious Greek forces at Salamis and Plataea which drove the Persians from Greek soil. The Greeks, as we know from their subsequent writings, saw their victory as the triumph of justice over injustice; of right over might. This theme of justice triumphing against injustice became themes of later Greek works: Herodotus's *Histories* and Thucydides's *Peloponnesian War*. Then came Plato's *Republic* and various other dialogues. It wasn't just history and philosophy that was touched by this concept of justice: *tisis* (τίσις). Drama concerned itself with this theme as well, inspired by those sublime events that secured Greek freedom against Persian imperial pretensions.

The Oresteia is a play that is concerned with the question of justice. In politics, justice may be the most pressing issue of any politeia. It is important to remember that in ancient Greece, despite attempts to find the roots of the public-private distinction in ancient Athens, such a clear division didn't exist (and we can argue today whether it does, in fact, exist or whether it remains a cherished myth we tell ourselves). The public impacts the private, the private cannot escape the public. Since public and private are intermixed, the kind of life we live—or have—is bound up with politics: life in the city. This is the best way to understand Aristotle's declaration that humans are political animals. We are more than mere social creatures seeking relations of love and intimacy. We live, eat, breathe, and die in the city—we exist in a realm touched by every facet of the political: law, economy, friendships and animosities, all exist under the roof of the polis.

The question of what kind of city we live in is not just Platonic, as I've written in understanding Plato's *Republic*, but equally artistic and dramatic.[*] The great plays of the Athenian playwright tradition deal with the same concern albeit in its dramatic, cathartic, form. As political animals, we must necessarily deal with the question of what kind of city we live in. Once we wrestle with that question, we can, hopefully, move toward the justice offered in a community united in religious, gender, political, and relational harmony. Amid the ruins of death and injustice, can life and justice—a new harmony of love—emerge? This is what *The Oresteia* attempts to reach, it is the best form of tragedy according to Aristotle's *Poetics*: the imitation of admirable things.

*

Agamemnon opens as if in a prison. The Watchman, an altogether insignificant character, begins: "Dear gods, set me free from all the pain, the long watch I keep, one whole year awake…propped on my arms, crouched on the roofs of Atreus like a dog." The beginning of the entire movement of the *Oresteia* is brilliantly set in motion by Aeschylus's opening. Something is not right, amiss, afoul. We have pain and dreariness, implications for a rough situation ahead. The chorus, rather extensive in the opening, sings of glory in slaughter: "Cry, cry for death, but good win out in glory in the end!" Let us remember this refrain of the chorus in *Agamemnon* vis-à-vis the ending chorus in the *Eumenides*.

---

[*]See my article, "Savagery, Irony, and Satire in Plato's Republic," *VoegelinView*, January 17, 2018.

Imprisonment, worry, fear, death, and slaughter. Quite the opening. From a tortured watchmen to a raucous chorus singing of the lust of violence, the play shifts to Clytemnestra—the equally tortured and vengeful wife of Agamemnon.

Agamemnon, mind you, has abandoned Clytemnestra in his glory seeking conquest that brought death and destruction to Troy. He has also sacrificed their daughter, Iphigenia, to secure safe passage and blessings in the war. Abandoned by her husband, who has also slaughtered their daughter to win glory in war, Clytemnestra is understandably angered by what she considers a great betrayal. In the absence of Agamemnon, she has taken a new lover— Aegisthus. Together, the two plot the downfall of Agamemnon upon his return.

Lies and deceit fill the House of Atreus. The glory of Mycenae, it is implied, is built on a crooked foundation that causes the apple to not fall far from the tree. The *parousia* of Agamemnon should have been his triumph. He was away for more than a decade. He is returning the conqueror and slaughterer of the east, vanquisher of the city of Troy. Clytemnestra even feigns the joy of his return when she exclaims, "[H]ave him come with speed, the people's darling – how they long for him. And for his wife, may he return and find her true at hall, just as the day he left her, faithful to the last." We know, however, that Clytemnestra speaks with the hissing tongue of lies. The reunion of a family long separated by war should mark the new harmony of life previously robbed by the chaos of war. The hopeful peace of the household is nevertheless ruptured by the bloodstained hand of vengeance.

Agamemnon returns but something is not right. Cassandra, a spoil of war, a princess of Troy taken captive to be a slave for Agamemnon, is hysterical. She serves a prophetess of destruction upon the House of Atreus. Cassandra's spasmodic utterances reveal the depravity of Agamemnon; moreover, she is a prisoner of horrid and cruel memories and a terrible lived experience that is foretelling the coming horrid cruelty and destruction of her captors. As the chorus sings after Cassandra's fateful screams, "Death is close, and quick."

Death does indeed come quick. Clytemnestra and Aegisthus hatch their plan to kill the King of Mycenae. The two lovers kill Cassandra and Agamemnon. Aegisthus sings: "O what a brilliant day it is for vengeance! Now I can say once more there are gods in heaven avenging men, blazing down on all the crimes of earth."

This returns us to the great theme of the *Oresteia* while also foreshadowing, with irony, the fate of Clytemnestra, Aegisthus, Orestes, and the gods. What is the difference between justice and vengeance? And what role do the gods play in upholding and dispensing justice? Are we prisoners of a violent fate, or do we have the power to enact justice in a world often filled with the violence of injustice?

At the end of *Agamemnon*, Clytemnestra reveals that they never sought justice but power: "You and I have power now. We will set the house in order once and for all." There is a temptation for political utopianism too, "We will set the house in order once and for all." Clytemnestra and Aegisthus trust in themselves. Whatever pieties they utter to the gods, whatever veil of justice they claim for themselves, is ultimately empty in their lust for power and political perfectionism.

*

The Libation Bearers opens with the contrast of our murderers several years after their heinous act. Orestes, who is now introduced to us, prays to the gods (specifically Hermes) for deliverance. Aeschylus immediately sets up Orestes as a model for piety for us. He is dutiful to the gods. As he is dutiful to the gods, he is also dutiful to his family, especially his father, however imperfect Agamemnon was. (Aeschylus doesn't paint a flattering picture of Agamemnon we must remember; Cassandra's delirious outbursts show him to be a monster and a monster he was.)

The chorus once again sings of the tension we suffer from: revenge or justice? The earth cries out for blood. The human heart seeks vengeance. Or does it seek justice? That dividing line is still obscured for us.

Enter Electra, the daughter of Agamemnon and Clytemnestra. The agony and suffering of Electra add a new dimension to the murder. Electra's suffering leads her to ask the audience to pity her. Through her pain, Aeschylus attempts to show the human consequences of murder. Human beings are not just bodily casualties. They are psychological casualties. Electra's agony is meant to illicit pity from the audience and softens us to Orestes's calculated movement toward vengeance/justice. The loving relationships that have been stolen from Electra are given a substitute between us (as audience) and her; a restored relationship of love emerges when Electra and Orestes are reunited which further drives the dramatic plot.

"Here I am. Look no further. No one loves you more than I," Orestes proclaims. "Your pain is mine. If I laugh at yours, I only laugh at mine," Orestes continues.

Electra, stumbling through the shock and joy, realizes her brother. "I turn to you the love I gave my mother – I despise her, she deserves it, yes, and the love I gave my sister, sacrificed on the cruel sword, I turn to you. You were my faith, my brother – you alone restore my self-respect."

Love in relationships, Aeschylus reveals in the touching interplay between Orestes and Electra, brings healing. It brings healing to the suffering wounds Electra has felt since Agamemnon's murder. It brings some healing to Orestes who is also without a family but now has—at the very least—Electra as a loving companion. Brother and sister share each other's pain and suffering in a beautiful moment of sibling love that brings a brief moment of solace in the midst of death and destruction.

Aeschylus does a wonderful job bringing a new depth to his characters and in the second act. In introducing Orestes as a pious son, we are filled with a sense of divine justice rather than human revenge emanating from his spirit. The deliverance of Electra's anguish in the reunion of brother and sister adds a sentimentality that was absent in the previous play. Murder is still to be done, but we have a new feeling within us. However cruel Agamemnon was, Clytemnestra and Aegisthus's murder of the king feels wrong. Orestes's murder of Clytemnestra and Aegisthus feels righteous. Or at least acceptable, understandable, justifiable. Aeschylus has gotten us to think about the nature of justice and revenge and where the distinction lay.

Furthermore, Aeschylus juxtaposes images and actions against each other. Just as Agamemnon is welcomed by a scheming Clytemnestra and Aegisthus and killed in this false hospitality, a scheming Orestes is welcomed by Clytemnestra and Aegisthus and puts on a veil of false hospitality to kill them. Just as Clytemnestra and Aegisthus murdered Agamemnon, so too does Orestes murder Clytemnestra and Aegisthus. Just as Clytemnestra and Aegisthus stood over and gloated above the dead body of Agamemnon, so too does Orestes stand over the dead bodies of his father's murderers. In this juxtaposition of imagery and action, imagery and actions that mirror one another, Aeschylus is probing the soul of justice and revenge, piety and hatred, love and lust.

Electra had called down divine retribution, "Both fists at once come down, come down – Zeus, crush their skulls. Kill! Kill!" As mentioned, the *Libation Bearers* opens with Orestes in prayer, "Hermes, lord of the dead, look down and guard the fathers' power. Be my saviour, I beg you, be my comrade now." These prayers are the only difference between Orestes and

Electra vis-à-vis Clytemnestra and Aegisthus. Aeschylus seemingly wants to assert that religious fidelity, piety, has something to do with justice. Prayers to the gods are conspicuously absent in the plotting of Clytemnestra and Aegisthus. Agamemnon is a bastard, this we know. Yet we are unsettled by his murder. Clytemnestra and Aegisthus are bastards too, but we are less unsettled by their murder. We hold Clytemnestra and Aegisthus in contempt. We hold Orestes in some degree of sympathy despite the continuation of bloodshed by his hands.

*

Cycles of violence dominate the course of the *Oresteia*. Violence begets violence. Orestes, after murdering Clytemnestra and Aegisthus, is haunted and hounded by the furies. He is driven into exile, chased by the spirits of the old world calling for death, revenge. He heads to Athens where Athena is the patron goddess, where Apollo is also an enshrined god. *The Eumenides*, then, is the resolution to the dark spell and retributive spirit of violence. The furies call for violence. Blood for blood. An eye for an eye and a tooth for a tooth. Orestes, in the presence of gods and goddesses of reason and justice, rationally pleads his case. The previous two acts have shown us the outcome of violent retribution moved by pure passion: murder. The furies call for vengeance, a perpetuation of murder. Orestes pleads his case, hoping to break the destructive spell of violence holding sway over us.

What makes the *Eumenides* a remarkable concluding act—given the fact that the fourth installment of the *Oresteia* is missing, and perhaps divinely so as it works exceptionally well as the concluding piece—is how action gives way to rationality, *logos* supersedes *energeia*. Looking back on the actions taken in *Agamemnon* and the *Libation Bearers*, and the action called for by the furies, there is no rule of law and courts of arbitration and justice. Pure will dominates. Now, however, will is tempered by rationality, by reason.

There is endless discussion as to the nature of the furies. Psychologically, they can be interpreted as the guilt-stricken conscience of Orestes in having murdered his mother. After all, the furies call for Clytemnestra's revenge, not Aegisthus's. Alternatively, the furies also represent the old law and the customs of ancient Greece. They are the manifestation of tradition, a tradition rooted in that retributive understanding of "justice," a perversion of justice, the call for vengeance. Moreover, the furies can also be seen as a manifestation of the human condition, the twists and turns, turbulence and turmoil, of the human life in its complex miseries. The call for revenge is always hanging over us. Literally. Some might say that the desire for vengeance that the furies shriek for is all too hauntingly natural.

So Orestes flees. As he flees he is hounded by the furies. He is a broken and shattered man, a tarnished son and brother, and exiled human, a tormented soul like all of us.

Yet Orestes retains that cloak of piety. Once more he cries out to the gods, Apollo in particular: "Lord Apollo, you know the rules of justice, know them well. Now learn compassion too. No one doubts your power to do great things." From first introduction to end of the play, Orestes is portrayed as having some sort of communion with the gods. This is not accidental on Aeschylus's part. While the images and sounds of death surround him, the images and sounds of life—the gods—are also nearby. They never desert him, or he never deserts them.

It is the gods who bring forth the revelation of life to us over the course of the play. The furies and their leader confront Apollo and demand justice. Or, more appropriately, revenge. Apollo strikes back. "Why, you'd disgrace – obliterate the bonds of Zeus and Hera queen of the brides. And the queen of love you'd throw to the winds at a word, disgrace love, the source of mankind's nearest, dearest ties. Marriage of man and wife is Fate itself, stronger than oaths, and Justice guards its life. But if one destroys the other and you relent – no revenge, not a glance in anger –then I say your manhunt of Orestes is unjust."

Apollo's revelation reveals what we have already been internally wrestling with from the time Orestes murdered Clytemnestra and Aegisthus. Grisly and gruesome as murder is, Orestes did so out of some fidelity to his father, his family; in other words, out of love. This stands in stark contrast to the naked power politics and desire of pure revenge exemplified by Clytemnestra and Aegisthus.

After Apollo's rebuke of the furies, Orestes comes to Athena and begs entrance in her presence. He declares himself free of blood guilt, of the murder he had committed which Apollo has defended. Prostrate before Athena, goddess of reason, wisdom, and justice, Orestes will plead his case.

The court trial between Orestes and the furies in Athena's presence is the climax of the play and the climax that the entire movement of the *Oresteia* has been building to. As mentioned, we are moving from the world of pure will and the id to rationality and the superego. The action that has driven the play so far is coming to a close as will is superseded by reason. Before the presence of almighty Athena, Orestes and the furies do battle—not with force of arms but with force of persuasion, with speech. Physical force, which was the manifestation of confrontation in the preceding plays, disappears as intellectual force, rationality and persuasion, take center stage.

During the court proceeding, Orestes is still clearly haunted by the murder of his mother. "The blood sleeps, it is fading on my hands, the stain of mother's murder washing clean. It was still fresh at the god's hearth. Apollo killed the swine and the purges drove it off. Mine is a long story if I'd start with the many hosts I met, I lived with, and I left them all unharmed. Time refines all things that age with time...Athena, help me!" Yet again we see Orestes in communion with the gods; as he pleads before Athena we have the imagery of a human co-laboring with the gods, human life is incomplete without the gods. Justice, then, is incomplete without the gods.

The furies, by contrast, link arms and dance and seek to bring force and terror into the proceeding. Revenge, the demand for blood reciprocity in murder, is declared to be the birthright they are seeking. "[W]e rise," they sing, "witness bound to avenge their blood we rise in flames against him to the end...This, this is our right, spun for us by the Fates, the ones who bind the world, and none can shake our hold."

*

Morality and justice can be horrifying realities when you first come to realize their existence. This is what shocks the furies before Athena. If cycles of violence only lead to more violence, and that this cycle of violence is exactly what the furies seek to perpetuate, the horror that one must feel when one recognizes another path—that of reconciliation rather than destructive violence—must be gut wrenching.

Athena asks where will the cycle of violence end? The leader of the furies declares "Where there is no joy." In other words, death. But death begets death.

Balance is needed. Athena's adjudication walks a tight rope; civilizational fragility is also a topic implicit in the trial. Civilization exists where there is a law and justice. Civilization dissipates where law and justice are eroded. Arguments over the moral law abound. Both Orestes and the furies claim to be guided by the moral law. But Orestes's moral law is the light of the day, the furies' the darkness of the night.

Aeschylus seems to posit that both are part of the human condition. This is what makes the furies sympathetic. Revenge is an all too human instinct. That is what the furies are crying out for. The desire for revenge in response to a callous act of murder. (Though they conveniently leave out the callous act of murder on the part of Clytemnestra whom they are representing from the grave.) Yet we also instinctively know that the base desire that the furies are governed by are inconducive to human, social, life. Revenge cannot allow life in the city to be fruitful. Id and superego are intertangled in a gruesome wrestling match. Superego, eventually, wins.

Athena rules in favor of Orestes not so much out of his devotion to filial piety, but out of a recognition that the cycle of violence must come to an end. Reason, persuasion, is therefore the superior law to will. Athena acknowledges that the furies are pursuing justice of some kind. She accosts them, however, for the manner in which they sought it: outside the law, outside of reason. Taking matters into one's own hands brings only bloodshed and destruction.

The furies are, appropriately, furious. They rebuke the Olympians. "You, you younger gods! – you have ridden down the ancient laws, wrenched them from my grasp – and I, robbed of my birthright, suffering, great with wrath, I loose my poison over the soil, aieee!" Athena calms the storm of the furies by articulating the necessity of persuasion against passion, of reason over will, "But if you have any reverence for Persuasion, the majesty of Persuasion, the spell of my voice that would appease your fury – Oh please stay."

Athena's taming of the furies represents the triumph of legal jurisprudence and civil law over the human instinct. The furies represent the boiling blood of human existence; they are the darkness to the day, that other side of human nature we like to ignore. But Aeschylus doesn't ignore it. He shows it in its naked brutality. But he also reveals how it can be tamed and brought into the services of the polity, of human life. Instinct and rage are powerful forces, but without the rule of law, which Athena is establishing, life would just be an endless cycle of bloodshed and violence. We must have calm, we must have peace, we must have harmony between day and night, between id and superego, between passion and persuasion.

The furies relent. They accept Athena's persuasion. The furies, we realize, have been the embodiment of the original chorus: "Cry, cry for death, but good win out in glory in the end." Now, however, in the end, they are singing a new song: "Cry, cry in triumph, carry on the dancing on and on. This peace between Athena's people and their guests must never end. All-seeing Zeus and Fate embrace, down they come to urge our union on – Cry, cry in triumph, carry on the dancing on and on!"

Aeschylus's achievement is enduring for several reasons. He recognizes the torn nature of humanity, between lust and love, between instinct and reason, between passion and persuasion. He doesn't so much abrogate one half for the other as much as he seeks to tame the darker side of human nature and subordinate it to what has been called "the better angels of our nature." Additionally, Aeschylus articulates through the *Eumenides* the importance of reason and persuasion to justice. Without reasoning and persuasion, courts of law and their legal arrangements are null and void. We are the inheritors of this ideal of justice. Furthermore, Aeschylus doesn't exile the furies into the abyss.

The furies are given an invitation to join in the co-creation of a better city. They accept. Enemies have become friends. Reconciliation, Aeschylus tells us, despite all the blood and hardships of the past, is possible. Reconciliation, rather than vengeance, ends the spell of violence and is the most reasonable, and just, action to pursue. For in reconciliation the possibility of love emerges. In reconciliation, rather than destruction, inclusion, rather than exclusion, true justice is manifested and the creation of a better city, a better republic, is possible. Two and half millennia later, we are still struggling to achieve that noble vision.

This essay was first published at *VoegelinView*, 10 January 2022.

Chapter 3

Antigone Agonistes

Aristotle defined the heart of tragedy as the imitation of admirable action in the *Poetics*. And among the Greek tragedians, Sophocles reigns supreme as the tragedian par excellence of Athens. As Matthew Santirocco wrote, "More than any other dramatist except perhaps Shakespeare, Sophocles is regarded as the quintessential tragedian." If so, and if Aristotle is right that the essence of tragedy is a teaching in admirable action, what is the admirable action that Antigone undertakes in her eponymous tragedy which ends in her death?

Antigone, as we know, follows its titular protagonist as she struggles against divided loyalties. Antigone's brothers have both recently been killed in civil war: Eteocles and Polyneices. Creon, honoring Etocles's patriotism, decides to honor his death at the exclusion of the treacherous Polyneices. Filial love is tested in Etocles's and Polyneices's death. The state, led by Creon, honors one brother while shunning the other; Antigone is caught between the love due to family members and the loyalty demanded by the state.

Sophocles, though a dramatist, was a political theorist. If not a political theorist, he certainly had much to say about politics.

The greatest of the tragedians, Sophocles sang in a chorus celebrating the Greek victory at Salamis over the Persians in 480 B.C. By the time of his death, Greece was at war with itself as the final campaigns of the Peloponnesian War were undertaken in 406 B.C. Sophocles's life spanned the golden age of Athens, its rise and fall, the sudden and spectacular emergence of Greece and its slip into decadence and downfall which would lead to the Hellenic city-states being overrun by Macedon in the next century.

Antigone, as far as we know, was written a decade before the outbreak of the Peloponnesian War. It was, therefore, written in a time of great political energy and transformation. The rise of the polis was now capturing the hearts and minds of the Greeks, especially the Athenians, who were moving away from the filial loyalties of the past toward the new collective citizenry offered in the emergent city-state democracies of the fifth century B.C. When one reads Plato and Aristotle, one might be struck by the limited discussion placed on clan, family, and tribe; unlike Near Eastern political theologies and cosmogonies which stressed such lineages, the great political philosophers of Greece emphasize the state and collective citizenship as the highest goods in political life (Aristotle, though, leaves more room for the family and property than does Plato but nevertheless exalts the importance of the state and citizenship above filial piety and devotion).

In this context of political and filial transformation, Sophocles wrote his many plays (of which only seven have survived to posterity). In *Antigone*, we see this tension between the old ways and the new and all-powerful state take center stage. Where will Antigone's heart be devoted?

The essence of *Antigone* is the struggle of the heart, of love; the battle between remaining loyal to the decrees of Creon (the state) and the demands of filial piety and burial (Polyneices). Antigone initially tries to find solace and comfort in the presence of her sister, Ismene, which hints at Antigone's predisposed disposition. She is an intimately filial individual seen through her want of affection from her sister. As Antigone says to Ismene when seeking her support in burying Polyneices against Creon's decree, "He is my brother still, and yours; though you would have it otherwise, but I shall not abandon him."

In declaring that Antigone will not abandoning Polyneices, Sophocles reveals to us in the opening moments of the play what the admirable action will be: Antigone's devoted heart to her brother. Against Antigone's devotion to her brother, Creon vocally declares the new political order at hand in Greece and the world: "I find intolerable the man who puts his country second to his friends. For instance, if I saw ruin and danger heading for the state, I would speak out. Never could I make my country's enemy my private friend, knowing as I do, she is the good ship that bears us safe."

Creon's role in the play is to serve as the mouthpiece of the new political zeitgeist. The state demands all loyalty; devotion to friends and family, as Creon says, cannot coexist with the demand of loyalty to the state which "bears us safe." It is even implied in Creon's statement that intense love for friends and family threatens the state. It is imperative, then, for the state to break those bonds and that is precisely what Creon sets out to achieve in his combative confrontation with Antigone.

Antigone defies Creon's order and ventures out the bury the body of Polyneices. She is discovered and accused by sentries as defying the laws of the state. Creon confronts her, "Come, girl, you with downcast eyes, did you or did you not, do this deed?" Antigone admits her actions, "I did. I deny not a thing."

Antigone and Creon argue over the morality/immorality of the state's decree. In the preceding chorus, the chorus had extoled the "rule of law" through Creon's dictatorial fiat. Fiat declaration is seemingly implied as the rule of law, even if it is arbitrarily enacted. In contrast to Creon's statism, Antigone defends the tradition of filial piety and the due reverence of burial rites (something very sacred to the Greeks). The agon, the conflict, is now fully brewing; the storm has been unleashed and is crashing down upon us as we witness this struggle of supremacy between the state (Creon) and filial devotion (Antigone). Antigone is condemned to die.

The conflict between state loyalty and filial loyalty is exacerbated with the entry of Haemon into the play. Haemon is the son of Creon and betrothed to Antigone whom he deeply loves. Initially it seems as if Haemon will cut Antigone loose, abandon her to her fate, and abide in loyalty to his father's— the state's—decision in condemning Antigone. However, Haemon begins to gently prod his father's hardened heart. He attempts to get Creon to spare Antigone. Father and son now erupt in vitriolic conflict toward each other.

Creon's outlook is fully revealed to us when he speaks to his son, "But as for anarchy, there is no greater curse than anarchy. It topples cities down, it crumbles homes, it shatters allied ranks in broken flight that disciple kept whole: For discipline preserves and orders well. Let us then defend authority and not be ousted by a girl." Here is the fullest maturation of Creon's disposition. He considers it his duty as king to defend the authority and order placed upon him by virtue of his rule. Furthermore, as Friedrich Hölderlin brought out in his translation, there also seems to be intergender tensions between Creon and Antigone; by law Haemon's marriage to Antigone will deprive Creon of an heir for the continuation of his bloodline's rule as Oedipus's bloodline is restored through the marriage of Haemon and Antigone. Yet Haemon says something wise in rebuke of the growing tyranny of his father. When Creon asserts that he, and he alone (not the mob) rules the state, Haemon rebuts by saying that singular rule is a cruel parody of the polis, "A one man state is no state at all." Creon snaps back, "The state is he who rules it."

Thus we see that Creon's motives are rooted in power. Antigone's motives are rooted in love. Sophocles plays this tension between power and love magnificently and poignantly. Like many greater thinkers after him, Sophocles seems to assert that power and love cannot coexist; that either power eviscerates love or love forsakes power. And power eviscerating the bonds of love is patently clear in Creon's case. Love forsaking power is also where the arc of Antigone's and Haemon's destinies move us to.

Creon against Antigone and Creon against Haemon reveals the corrosive and acidic power that statism brings into relationships. Creon, as Antigone's uncle, loses his relationship with his niece because of the quarrel. Creon, as Haemon's father, also loses his relationship with his son because of their infighting. Creon's headstrong rule destroys the very fabric which had given his life meaning.

Let us return, briefly, to why Antigone is a heroine. Although a descendant of noble blood, Antigone as a woman of royal lineage in the confines of royal expectations is very much at the mercy of the political powers that be. If her father were still alive, she would likely be utilized as political capital for Oedipus's political designs. Though Oedipus is gone, she is still, in some sense, a pawn to Creon's political machinations. Power, once again, deprives one of love.

Antigone's heroism is found in her agency, an agency moved by love which compels her to defy her uncle, the King of Thebes, and draws her closer to her dead brother to bury his body with the funeral rites he deserves as a Greek and as sanctioned by the moral law of the gods. Antigone's freedom is found in her choice to honor the natural law of filial devotion rather than the arbitrary decrees of the state embodied in the person of Creon. In defying the state, Antigone reveals the totality of freedom: freedom found only in love. Love breaks the power of the state which is why it is dangerous; Creon's fear of "anarchy" masks what he truly fears: lack of devotion to the state. He would rather the people be subjects than citizens, slaves than lovers. Antigone's heroic action is found in the supremacy of the heart refusing to be curtailed by the force of the state.

So too is Haemon's freedom found in love instead of power. He breaks free of his father and chases after Antigone to declare his undying love for her. In Haemon's love for Antigone, he too escapes the clutches of his father's desires. Love, and love alone, Sophocles begins to reveal to us, sets us free.

But *Antigone* is a tragedy. Sophocles, as a Greek, did not have the mature revelation of love as a salvific force which was inherited by the West through the adoption of Christianity. The notion that "love wins" is thoroughly

Christian, though we might say that love frees us is something undeniably found in Greek literature albeit with a tragic caveat.

Sophoclean love draws us to death, but it is a death that we face with dignity and liberty rather than degradation and enslavement. We are not slaves to death. We can stare death in the face with a dignity of soul unrivaled by other mortal creatures. If death is certain, we can at least face it with dignity and freedom. Antigone's lament crystalizes this reality for us:

> Come tomb, my wedding chamber, come!
> You sealed off habitations of the grave!
> My many family dead, finished fetched
> in final muster to Persephone.
> I am last to come, and lost the most of all,
> my life still in my hands.
> And yet I come (I hope I come) toward a father's love,
> beloved by my mother,
> And by you, my darling brother, loved.
> Yes, all of you,
> Whom these hands have washed, prepared and sped.

Antigone's lament reveals the warmth and spirit of her heart. She is a woman free to make the choice of death by love. She accepts Creon's criminalization of love and doesn't flinch; she doesn't forsake love for the false life offered in the body politic. She gives up her power as a noble princess to die having honored her brother and her familial bonds. In her love, Antigone is led away with dignity as Creon and his guards arrest her for her crime of love and take her to a cavern cell as punishment.

Now let us return to Creon. Having just hauled away Antigone to die, Creon begins to suffer from guilt over his actions. Two of his nephews have been slain in civil war. He has just condemned his niece to death. And his son has deserted him over his strongarm tyrannical politics. Creon, a man who was once surrounded by friends and family, is isolated and alone despite the sublime power he wields.

The encounter with the blind prophet Tiresias is the return to Creon's moral sensibilities, a return to the moral law of the gods whom Tiresias says are unhappy with Creon's actions. The displeasure of the gods, the awakening of the moral law inside Creon, causea an abrupt change of heart in the tyrant's disposition. When Creon exclaims, "My mind's made up. I'll not be slow to let her loose myself who locked her in the tomb. In the end it is the ancient codes—oh, my regrets!—that one must keep: To value life then one must value law." The "ancients codes" and "life" and "law" that Creon speaks of is the love of family which he had scorned in his tyrannical pronouncements.

Alas, it is too late for Creon. He has learned the truth about the order of the world, the truth that had always been known to Antigone and chosen by Haemon in his rebuke of the tyranny of his father in favor of his love for Antigone. Creon rushes to free Antigone only to learn that she has committed suicide. Inside the cave, Creon sees Haemon lamenting over Antigone's dead body.

The two come to blows as Haemon blames Creon for this sorrowful lot in life and attempts to stab him (the final dissolution of their relationship which moved from verbal sparring to physical violence); Creon manages to escape. Haemon, then, turns the blade on himself to die with Antigone than live alone. In a touching scene revealing the power of love and how it binds souls together, Sophocles writes of this unity in death: "And conscious still but failing, limply folded Antigone close into his arms—Choking blood in crimson jets upon her waxen face. Corpse wrapped in love with corpse he lies, married not in life but Hades: Lesson to the world that inhumane designs Wreak a havoc immeasurably inhumane."

Moreover, Eurydice, Creon's wife, also commits suicide upon hearing the news of Haemon's death. Creon's world has come crashing down over him. He may still be King of Thebes, but he has lost everything that is so precious, so dear, truly meaningful, in life. The lust for power which Creon had embodied only led to misery, death, and loneliness. The King of Thebes is now isolated, alienated, alone in the world.

Sophocles has shown us to alternative visions of life. The life of power leads to misery, death, and loneliness. The life of love, impetuous as it may be, leads to unity and relationships. Antigone retained a communion with Polyneices despite his death; Haemon retained a communion with Antigone despite her death. Antigone took Polyneices in her arms to bury him. Haemon took Antigone in his arms to die with her in love. Creon, meanwhile, loses everything.

While the choral ode concludes by asserting wisdom can be found in suffering, the suffering that Creon now embodies having lost his family, the play ends with a moment of moral instruction to the audience about what matters in life and what ancient codes and laws of life we are to follow. This returns us to Aristotle and his assertion that the heart of tragedy is the imitation of admirable action. If Aristotle is right that tragedy attempts to inspire admirable action from among its audience, what is the admirable action that Sophocles wanted to leave us with in *Antigone*, one of the grandest and most poignant tragedies of the Athenian literary tradition?

It is undoubtedly that our first and primary loyalty is the love due to family rather than the state. Even if it brings death, the choice of love rather than power is the most heroic thing a human can choose. In choosing love over power we are truly free and can meet death with dignity and a spirit of inspiration that will live on forever.

This essay was first published by *The Imaginative Conservative*, 2 November 2021.

Chapter 4

Euripides: Oracle of Modernity

"Cry, cry in triumph, carry on the dancing on and on. This peace between Athena's people and their guests must never end. All-seeing Zeus and Fate embrace, down they come to urge our union on—Cry, cry in triumph, carry on the dancing on and on!" That is how Aeschylus ended his *Oresteia* trilogy. The furies, which had so hounded and haunted Orestes, had transformed into co-laborers with Athena singing and dancing for the joy of reason and civilization. Euripides, the great cynic and blasphemer, took a darker and starker approach to the gods and Greek civilization—perhaps one of the reasons why he was less successful than his predecessors in being awarded at festivals and competitions for his writing.

The Bacchae is a classic cornerstone of Western literature. It is the one play of Euripides's that is part of the undisputed classical canon, though *Medea*, *Iphigenia in Aulis*, and the *Trojan Women* are also masterpieces and should be read to get a fuller portrait of Euripides.

The Failure of Reason and the Fall of Athena

Euripides wrote in an anxious and transformative age. The Persians had just been defeated and Athens, Athena, had ascended as the premier power among the Greeks. Euripides was but a young man when Athens ascended to her infamous glory that still mesmerizes—and haunts—our civilization. The Athenian empire, as recounted by Thucydides in his *History of the Peloponnesian War*, was exceptional because it was not the product of conquest but of mutual defense. No other empire, the Athenian delegates argue, had ever been formed in such a manner.

But the later plays of Euripides, including his *Bacchae*, are set in dire and dark times. Athens' grand Sicilian conquest had failed. The Peloponnesian War had turned against Athens. And the city was suffering from civil war, sexual depravity, and the general disintegration of its society. Euripides might be reaching back to ancient and mythological figures, but their tales and fates are eerily similar to the Athens at the end of the fifth century on the eve of the death of Euripides. The darkness of Euripides's tragedies coincides with the nadir of Athenian grandeur. It is well known that many of his plays composed during the Peloponnesian War (like the *Trojan Women*) are veiled commentaries on the state of Athenian society and the war itself.

The Athens celebrated by Athena and the transformed furies at the end of Aeschylus's *Eumenides*—and the Athens eulogized by Pericles in Thucydides's *History of the Peloponnesian War*—is not the Athens that Euripides composed his late plays to reflect. The *Bacchae*, among the last of Euripides's plays, was composed in a tumultuous city filled with strife and conflict. And though the play is set in Thebes, the tragedy that befalls Pentheus is an esoteric commentary on the state of Athenian society and the insufficiency of the gods of the city.

Athena is the goddess of wisdom, of reason and persuasion, alongside being a strong goddess of war. But her wisdom and justice are what primarily define her. And that her name is bore by Athens—Athens is supposed to be the wise and just city in mirror reflection of its patron deity which exonerated Orestes and transformed the furies.

Something wicked comes to Greece. This is the reality of the situation when the *Bacchae* opens. Dionysus travels in from the eastern lands. Dionysus, though a nominally Greek god, is presented, by Euripides, as if a foreign oriental sex god. Moreover, the power of Dionysus is immediately made known to the crowd, or reader: "I come from Lydia, its territories teeming with gold; and from rich Phrygia. I am all-conqueror in the sun beaten steppes of Persia, the walled cities of Bactria, the wintry lands of Media, and in Arabia Felix—land of the blest. All Asia is mine, and along the fringes of the sea, the pinnacled glory of all those mingled cities of Greeks and many races." Everywhere Dionysus goes he "conquer[s]." No land, whether south, east, north, or, now, west, can escape the consuming madness of Dionysus, Bacchus, and the Bacchants.

We may have now forgotten, but it certainly wasn't lost on fifth century Athenians, that dancing is an intrinsically sexual act. Dancing is the great rite, the grand ritual, that Dionysus brings with him. As Dionysus proclaims, "Elsewhere, everywhere, I have established my sacraments and dances, to make my godhead manifest to mortals." Elsewhere indeed, the chorus which lauds over Dionysus sings: "For sacred dances and joy…In the mountains the wild delight of Bacchus in his soul. His ritual he undergoes: Cybele's orgies, great Mother's, He shakes the thyrsus on high."

The women of Thebes are entranced, as if sex slaves, by this new god and his rituals. They lose their cloths and their minds, dancing and howling wildly on the mountain at night. The social order of the city is so threatened that Pentheus orders Dionysus arrested and his men prepare for battle to put an end to this threat. Pentheus, as the King of Thebes, has a duty to protect his citizens and the social fabric (and order) of his civilization which he, correctly, perceives to be threatened by the arrival of Dionysus.

It is now well accepted that Euripides did not have a change of heart late in life. Euripides had always been critical of the gods. He was, at the eve of his death, still critical of the gods.

Moderns may be sympathetic to Dionysus, but Dionysus is hardly presented in any sympathetic light by Euripides. Euripides sees little good in Dionysus after he viciously and brutally turns on Pentheus, intoxicating the king who giggles like a girl and dresses like a woman to get a better view of the naked women of the city in their entranced ritual dancing and moaning. Pentheus, however, is not without fault. But as the play reaches its climax, we grieve for Pentheus, his mother, and his grandfather, but hardly shed a tear for Dionysus. In fact, we turn on Dionysus and wish to tear him limb from limb just as the Titans had done to him.

The contemporary reading of fun-loving Dionysus against power imposing Pentheus misses the obvious and more contextual reality of the play.

Both Dionysus and Pentheus are engaged in an exercise of power and will and not "freedom vs. tyranny" as post-World War II readings tend to now assert. Pentheus may have acted with impiety toward this foreign oriental sex god, but Pentheus certainly had the foresight, as the play reveals by his grisly dismemberment at the hands of the women of the city—including his own mother—of the threat that Dionysus posed. In Pentheus challenging Dionysus, the king is not challenging the free-loving and free-playing Dionysus but challenging Dionysus's lust for control and power. After all, when Dionysus is introduced, he proclaims his power of conquest and that all the world, sans Hellas, has been brought under his dominion.

The contest between Pentheus and Dionysus is one of power. Pentheus understands the arrival of this foreign sex-crazed god as a threat to his power but also the power and social order of Thebes. Dionysus, in seeing Pentheus's seriousness in gathering his armies for battle and clearing out the mountains of the Bacchants, understands that his power is being threatened by Pentheus. Sacrilege and impiety are mere pretexts to kill the king, which is precisely what Dionysus concludes must happen for his power—not his free-loving and free-playing spirit—to survive. Irrespective of the reception and development of Dionysus in the subsequent tradition, the Dionysus of Euripides is a cold, lustful, and power-hungry dark god of vindictive cruelty. Dionysus is a god of dark fear and manipulation; his dark presence fills Pentheus with fear and, when Pentheus challenges Dionysus's arrival, he manipulates the king to be torn limb from limb by his induced dancers.

Euripides's gods are not the gods of Aeschylus though they bear the same name. No, Euripides's gods are the gods of Hesiod given a new, cunning, and manipulative makeover. Furthermore, they are depicted as clear threats to the human social order. At least Hesiod's gods fought among themselves and castrated the bodies and organs of fellow immortals instead of ripping humans limb from limb with their entrails spilling out into the laps of fanatically enraptured servants.

Dangerous Gods, Dangerous Love, and Tragic Humans

It seems to me that Euripides is a great and scandalous humanist as well as being morally astute to the problems concerning human relationships. Aeschylus's human progress is still controlled by the gods, as indicated by Athena's role at the end of the *Eumenides*. We labor with the gods and appeal to the gods in Aeschylus, but the gods have the final say.

Euripides's human progress—if there is progress in his tragedies—is not in the hands of the gods but in the hands of humans. Pentheus is brutally torn apart by the women of Thebes who, once freed from Dionysus's licentious spell, realize the depravity of their actions and mourn for him. Euripides, through Agave and the chorus, remind us of the brutality and harshness of the world, especially the classical pantheon whose gods raped, murdered, and controlled others at whim.

Dionysus, in standing over the dismembered body of Pentheus, and observing the tragic scene of a man's mother holding her son's head as if a lion's head, defends himself by asserting that Pentheus's impiety justified his death: "The sins of jealousy and anger made this Pentheus deal unjustly with one bringing blessings, whom he disgracefully imprisoned and assaulted." But what blessings did Dionysus bring? Slavery and insanity are what Dionysus wrought. Indeed, Cadmus falls to his knees in slavery to Dionysus crying out: "Have mercy Dionysus, we have sinned." But who brought forth the sin of filicide? Dionysus, not Pentheus or Agave. Agave's final words are: "Let others meddle with Bacchants." In tearing her son apart in a crazed stupor, Agave, apparently, has had enough of being a Bacchant dancer and has returned to her senses and wants nothing to do with the god who caused her to tear her son apart like a crazed beast.

It is the human characters who have—and manifest—moral realization in the play, not Dionysus. Cadmus awakens Agave and the women from their intoxication to see the horror and suffering they have wrought to poor Pentheus. Agave and the women take responsibility for their actions and weep for the king. In mournful exodus, it is the humanity of the Thebans freed from Dionysus which touches us most in this bleak and dark tragedy that W.B. Yeats recalled as if peering into the hollow sacristy to see the secretive and horrifying sacrament of a blood thirsty god made flesh to feast on the flesh of his victims. During the introduction to *The Trojan Women*, Euripides also presents Athena and Poseidon as conniving and jealous gods—making a pact to make the return journey of the Greeks as miserable as possible (even though Athena had fought on the side of the Greeks).

Though composed 25 years earlier than the *Bacchae*, Euripides's *Medea* deals with this same theme of gods or humans for control of our destinies and dispositions. Medea has been slighted by Jason and her life and social standing has all been swept out from under her feet. Her brutal murder of her own sons is unforgivable. But Jason is equally not without any guilt. The gods are absent in this play but not without being invoked.

The rage of Medea brings death and destruction. The infidelity of Jason brings rage leading to death and destruction. In the second choral ode, Euripides tells us something scandalously shocking—at least in comparison to where Greek literature had been progressing up to his moment in time: "Love is a dangerous thing, Loving without any limit. Discredit and loss it can bring." Love has entered the consciousness and vocabulary of the Greek literary-philosophical tradition in large part thanks to Homer and Aeschylus. However, love in Euripides is scorned, shown to be hollow, and ultimately something "dangerous."

Moreover, love is also deconstructed throughout Euripides's plays. The emphasis placed on love, as was the case with Medea, only came back to haunt her—indeed, love made her a slave and did not bring her salvation but cheaply disposed of her when socially and politically relevant.

Euripides's plays show us the hollowness and vanity, indeed, the cruelty of the gods. Athena has been dethroned, and the empty gods who demand child sacrifices and capture entire cities and make them servile slaves have returned. Humans have once again been deprived of light and made into the toiling servants of the gods whose cruel fates and sadistic impulses can visit us at any time. Moreover, love is also deconstructed throughout Euripides's plays. The emphasis placed on love, as was the case with Medea, only came back to haunt her—indeed, love made her a slave and did not bring her salvation but cheaply disposed of her when socially and politically relevant. (This too is true in the *Trojan Women* where the love exhibited by Hecuba and Andromache for a now burnt Troy and their slain husbands add to their misery.)

Are the gods worthy of veneration? In answering this question we must ask, *which gods?* The Greek gods went through many faces though they bore the same names. The gods born from Hesiod's pen were cruel and lust-filled gods who engaged in patricide and usurpation. The gods of Homer are equally mischievous though Homer humanizes eros and gives us great hope as he shifts our concentration away from the gods and to fated human beings. The gods of Aeschylus are just and persuasive, rational and loving, gods we can relate with and ultimately become co-laborers with; Aeschylus provides the synthesis of the hateful gods of Hesiod and the fatalistic but humanistic love of Homer. The gods of Euripides are brutal, ruthless, and full of cruel surprises —the exact opposite of Aeschylus's gods or the beautiful and sumptuously fleshy gods of the Catholic Renaissance painters. The gods of Euripides are bloodthirsty and call for virgin sacrifices to procure blessing in war.

Nevertheless, Euripides was a moralist. But he was not locating the heart of morality in the gods, the cosmos, or even in other humans. Euripides located the heart of morality in ourselves—as individuals free from the bonds of the gods (and yes, even other persons). If we do find equally moral people where love can flourish, as Andromache did with Hector, that is no guarantee of the good life either—just look at what happened to Andromache after Hector's death and the sack of Troy and the agonizing pain Andromache subsequently suffered!

In this respect, Euripides was the first, and most dramatic, libertarian in Western history. We must look after ourselves and take responsibility for our actions. Only in accepting responsibility for ourselves and our actions can we have a social order worthy of being venerated and protected. The ultimate message of Euripides is the same message that Aristophanes has him speak in the *Frogs*: Be weary of trusting others for your salvation. That message has reverberated down through history ever since Euripides put it to dramatic form. In so many ways, Euripides was the oracle of modernity.

This essay was first published by *Merion West*, 19 August 2019.

Chapter 5

Euripides: Prophet of Pity

The acme of Euripides's literary genius coincided with the Peloponnesian War. As such, it isn't surprising that his later plays deal with war, slavery, and sexual degeneracy—all things that had devastated the once splendid city. *Electra, Hecuba, Andromache, The Trojan Women,* and *Iphigenia in Aulis* are all set during the Trojan War. Euripides isn't so much depreciating the heroic ideal of that war as much as he is providing extensive social commentary on the consequences of the Peloponnesian War as the long-ago war in Euripides's plays parallels the ongoing one devastating Greece. Moreover, his war plays examine who suffers most from the horrors of war and what becomes of humans as a result. His plays are, therefore, esoteric commentaries on the tragic consequences of the Peloponnesian War as well as reflections on the importance of pity to bring healing and peace to a battered and bloodied world.

*

Euripides was no proto-feminist though contemporary feminist readings often misconstrue the gynocentric nature of his plays. Euripides often depicted women as nymphomaniacs and Aristophanes satirized this side of Euripides in *Thesmophoriazusae.* However, Euripides was not without a strong sense of empathy for the plight of women. After all, it is from his pen that we see the plight of women in war. Euripides's plays are meant to shock his audience into pity, thus making him the great tragic playwright of pity in the Greek world.

The Trojan Women was written on the eve of the gambit which would ultimately bring about the downfall of Athens: the Sicilian Expedition. Athens' current moment in history, then, mirrored that of the Argives—a sea expedition for a faraway conquest. The play may have very well been an appeal for peace. After all, Euripides loathed war and exposed its naked hollowness in his plays which do not focus on the Trojan War itself but its disastrous consequences for those involved.

In the war plays a haunting image recurs: the separation of child from mother—from her arms or womb—which ends in death. Astyanax is ripped from the arms of Andromache. Iphigenia releases herself from the warm arms of her mother. Polyxena is also taken away from Hecuba. In its more brutal form, Agave butchers her own son at the dramatic conclusion of the *Bacchae*, and Medea slaughters her children after having smothered them in a coldly affectionate embrace.

*

Iphigenia's death, her separation from her mother, is the most noble—in some sense—of the child sacrifices that Euripides depicts in his various war tragedies. *Iphigenia in Aulis* conveys the image of a voluptuous woman being whisked away by lustful force. In his opening monologue, Agamemnon speaks of how the Greek army had assembled at Aulis. "He fell in love. She fell in love, and he carried her off to his ranch in the Idan hills," Agamemnon says, referring to the elopement of Paris and Helen. Helen is taken away from the bedchambers and arms of Menelaus, thus sparking the Trojan War.

Or was it?

The third choral ode reminds us of the lust-infested environment of the Trojan War. Helen is the offspring of a rape. She is the daughter of Leda, thanks to the advances of Zeus. The chorus of women sing of the doom that has befallen Troy and its women: "All this because you, Helen, child of Leda and the arch-necked swan. If the story they tell is true that the swan was really Zeus; or is this only fable culled from poetic annals not worth knowing?"

The master ironist ends with a poetic twist. Is it important to know the fable of Helen's birth by rape? Euripides suggests that it is. In fact, omitting the fact that Helen was the child of such sexual violence depreciates the context and recurring images of lustful violence in Euripides's play. Not only is Helen taken away by Paris by force, but Helen herself was the offspring of a forceful advances of a high god onto a princess. Lust knows no boundaries; likewise, war knows no boundaries. What was conceived in lust will bring lust and, ultimately, misery.

Even Agamemnon, hardly an upstanding and noble figure, speaks an ironic truth when he says, "The Greek is possessed by a kind of lust to sail at once to this foreign land and put an end to the raping of Greek wives. They will kill my daughters in Argos. They will kill you and me if I break my pact with Artemis."

It is true that Agamemnon had vowed to sacrifice his virgin daughter to procure safe passage to Troy as atonement for killing the sacred deer of Artemis, but Agamemnon's words near the conclusion of the play also reveal the contradictions surrounding Helen's departure from Greece to Troy and the central role of lust in inciting the Trojan War. Earlier he had said she had fallen in love with Paris and seemingly joined with him on her own free will. Here, Agamemnon reveals the darker and older account of Helen's forceful abduction by the deviant Paris. Helen, though, is not without blame.

The circumstances surrounding her persona is one of unmitigated sexual lust, be it with Menelaus or Paris. Perhaps this is fitting given that she was born of Zeus's uncontrollable sexual appetite. In any case, Euripides subtly reveals that the Trojan War was born from rape: first, the rape of Leda by Zeus, which gave birth to Helen; second, the rape of Helen by Paris, which is implied when he says that the Greek army is intent on ending the "raping of Greek wives."

When Achilles returns to speak with Clytemnestra after having failed to persuade the Greek soldiers to release Iphigenia, the "uproar among the troops" reveals that in lust there can be no marriage or family. In the violence wrought by lust there can only be blood and bruises. Achilles was earlier introduced as a gullible, hot-rod boyfriend. His hair, body, and armor shined and dazzled all. He was the image of beauty and perfection. Returning to Clytemnestra he is bruised and soiled in dirt and mud. He barely escaped with his life.

Achilles's hatred toward Agamemnon has been well-known ever since Homer recounted their rivalry in the *Iliad*. If Euripides's account of the feud between the two great Argive heroes of the Trojan War is true, then Achilles had been Agamemnon's unwitting pawn, and it is understandable why he hates Agamemnon. Clytemnestra and Iphigenia were under the impression that the now eligible daughter was to be wed and believed Achilles to be the chosen groom. Achilles, when it was earlier revealed that Agamemnon had used his name to deceive Iphigenia, was outraged, "No, King Agamemnon has insulted me. He should have asked my permission if he wanted to use my name to trap his child. It was my name that made Clytemnestra bring her to him."

Yet Achilles's outrage is somewhat ambiguous. It seems like vanity is the primary reason for Achilles's rage. He was distraught that his name would forever be tarnished as the lure of the innocent Iphigenia to her death. He doesn't seem to have that much concern for Iphigenia initially, though he somewhat haphazardly redeemed himself in his attempt to save Iphigenia from the bloodlust of the army.

The atmosphere of deceit, lust, and rape is what makes the ending of the play so tragic but so powerful. Iphigenia willingly becomes the innocent sacrifice. Up to this point we have been reminded of constant misconduct and rape. Zeus raped Leda. Paris abducted Helen. Agamemnon deceived his family. In the midst of this storm that would make even Lucifer smile, Iphigenia—that white-cloaked, ruddy-faced, flowery-haired woman—stands out as the only truly noble individual in the play.

This does not make her death and separation from Clytemnestra less tragic. It serves to magnify our rage at Agamemnon who tries to rationalize his actions and present himself as a helpless and hapless man forced to do what he did by the gods. Agamemnon refuses to take responsibility for his actions, and really no one takes responsibility for his or her actions throughout the play. The chaos can only be remedied by the one heroine who takes responsibility for her actions and assumes the responsibilities of others. That is what makes her separation from Clytemnestra so touching and moving.

But we should not become so attached to Iphigenia's heroic self-sacrifice which allowed the Greeks to safely journey and lay waste to Troy. That is not Euripides's point. Instead, he wanted to show the hollowness of war itself and the tragic sacrifice of innocent victims, often virgin women.

Indeed, war and sacrifice go together, a fact which only intensifies the barbarism of war. Why did Iphigenia have to die? To secure the safe voyage of the Greek army who in a decade-long war would cause the deaths of thousands. The sacrifice of Iphigenia did not bring an end to death. It only served to bring further death. The haunting image of a fertile daughter being sacrificed for the end of war is the most scandalous image that Euripides can produce to reveal the horrifying reality of war: It is the coming-of-age daughters who suffer most from war.

*

What makes Iphigenia's death stand apart from the other children torn from the arms of their mothers is that hers is willing. (Though Euripides also writes a play in which Iphigenia survives, perhaps in part due to her nobility in bearing the wrongful misdeeds and irresponsibility of all parties involved in her death.) The same cannot be said for the screaming Astyanax when he is torn from the loving arms of Andromache in *The Trojan Women*.

Like *Iphigenia in Aulis*, *The Trojan Women* gives a contradictory account of Helen's role in the origin of the Trojan War. Nevertheless, lust still permeates the environment—at least concerning Helen's role in bringing misery to Hecuba, Andromache, and the litany of other Trojan widows who are now suffering under the tyrannical yoke of concubinal slavery. As the Leader says, "Troy, unhappy Troy, where so many thousands of young men were lost all for one woman's sake, one wanton lust!"

The death of Astyanax is a haunting image. Astyanax runs back to Andromache and hides in the comfort of her arms. Talthybius, the reluctant pawn of violence, wrenches Astyanax from Andromache's comforting and loving arms. As he tears Astyanax away, the boy screams in pain and sorrow, and he is flung from the battlements of Troy. Such a spectacle on stage must have struck the heart of the Greek audience who fancied themselves the pinnacle of civilization and humanity. But Euripides mocks this self-conception of exceptionalism as Andromache yells at the Greek soldiers, "You barbarians, what un-Greek cruelties can you invent? Must you kill a child—wholly innocent?"

After throwing Astyanax from the walls headfirst, the Greek soldiers return carrying him on a shield. At first glance one might think that the Greeks are treating his deceased and mangled body with a certain respect and honor. They have, after all, brought him back on a shield to his mother for a burial. They have even washed him clean of the blood and dirt. But the evidence of bruises and mangled limbs makes the image of Astyanax on the shield a cruel mockery of a sleeping child.

But the mother is absent for the return. She has been sold into slavery to Neoptolemus. Instead, it is Hecuba who is present to receive the bruised and battered corpse of Astyanax. She weeps in place of Andromache and says, "It is not you but I, your grandmother, an old cityless, childless crone, that has to bury your torn body. Wasted, lost forever, all those cuddles, all that care, all that watching you while you sleep."

Euripides's literary genius is revealed in Hecuba's lament. He links the image of the dead Astyanax on the shield to the image of the peacefully sleeping Astyanax with Andromache watching over him. Neither can share each other's love anymore. This image moves the audience to tears as Hecuba embraces the lifeless body of her grandson.

In *The Trojan Women*, Hecuba is presented as a pitiable woman who has had everything torn away from her. Her surviving daughters are sold into slavery or killed. Andromache, more a daughter to Hecuba than Helen ever was, is also carried away into slavery. The theme of virgin desolation remains: Earlier in the play, the Greeks snatch Cassandra away from Hecuba. Hecuba laments, "I saw my virgin daughters, bred for bridegrooms of the highest rank, torn from my arms and all their breeding thrown to foreigners."

Euripides's plays depict war without a romantic overcoat and with all its shocking tragedies. Children are separated from mothers—into captivity or death—in the most gruesome and barbaric way.

*

The eponymous play *Hecuba* continues the ruin of Priam's pitiable wife. Cassandra and Andromache have been taken away. Astyanax is dead. Now Polyxena, Hecuba's last remaining daughter, is to be torn away from her. Polyxena prophesies her own death to Hecuba:

> Pitiable woman, you will see me, your pitiable whelp, like a heifer bred in the mountains, torn from your arms and sent down to Hades with my throat cut, to the darkness under the earth, where I, unhappy Polyxena, shall lie among the dead.

Hecuba has nothing but hatred for Helen. This hatred is motivated by her love for Troy, for her dead children and husband, and for Polyxena. When Odysseus breaks the news of Polyxena's fate, Hecuba implores Odysseus to kill Helen:

> [Achilles] should have asked for Helen to be slaughtered at his grave. She brought him to his destruction at Troy… I beseech you not to tear my daughter from my arms. Do not kill her. We have dead bodies enough. This girl is my delight. In her I forget my sorrows. She is my comfort and takes the place of many things. She is my city, my nurse, my staff, my guide.

It is worthy to note that Hecuba associates her last surviving daughter with her city. Homer says that the bad man is he who is "lost to the clan, lost to the hearth, lost to the old ways, that one who lusts for all the horrors of war." In a heart-wrenching moment, Hecuba offers herself as a substitute on the sacrificial pyre so that Polyxena may live.

But Hecuba's offer of replacement is good enough for the Greeks. Polyxena must be sacrificed. In another scene that moves the heart but provokes shock and rage, Polyxena kisses her mother goodbye:

No, my dear mother, give me your sweet hand, and let me press my cheek to yours. For never again shall I look upon the radiant circle of the sun. This is the final time. You are listening to my last words. O my mother who gave me birth, I am going away to the Underworld.

Polyxena is subsequently taken away and killed at the grave of Achilles where her blood pours over his tomb.

Euripides portrays the further ruin of Hecuba: from a truly "pitiable woman" to a ravenous dog. He does so not to shun Hecuba for her own barbaric revenge on Polymestor, the killer of her youngest son, Polydorus, but to demonstrate the shocking consequences of war. Hecuba transforms from a "most unhappy woman" to a "dog with fire-red eyes" because she has been "lost to clan, lost to the hearth, lost to the old ways" and finally consumed by "the horrors of war." The descent of Hecuba is truly tragic: Having lost her family and fatherland, she becomes a murderer like those barbarous Argives.

The play opens in the tent of Agamemnon's captives. A specter of death looms over the play as Polydorus's ghost is the first character to speak. Of course, the play ends in death when Hecuba and the captive women blind Polymestor and kill his sons. That which began in captivity and death ends in captivity and death. When we are slaves to war, we become conduits of death.

*

Euripides's war plays center on women. Iphigenia, Hecuba, Andromache, Cassandra, Polyxena, and Helen all feature prominently. This concentration on the suffering of women, as well as children, reveals the bleak truth that war is most destructive to women. We see virgin brides sacrificed and murdered. We see mothers and grandmothers deprived of the fruits of their womb. We even see a woman who once asked innocent children to be spared become a killer of innocent children when she loses her family, hearth, and homeland.

Euripides doesn't romanticize war. He exposes its horror and bloodshed and shows us, bleakly and starkly, war's damaging effects on humans. We mustn't forget that Euripides composed the plays during the Peloponnesian War. Responding to the great bloodshed of young men, women, and virgins, Euripides's dramatic tragedies call for peace.

It is hard to ascertain whether Euripides really saw the family as important as Sophocles or Aristotle do. But what is clear is that war destroys families. The death of Astyanax, the culling of the womb, is evidence of that.

To Euripides who experienced the carnage of war, those who glorify and romanticize war are often men who have never loved and never had a family. Euripides lost his own son, Xenophon, in 429 B.C. at the outbreak of hostilities between Athens and Sparta. The loss of his son in war undoubtedly prompted his sentiments toward women. A society that is enslaved by war is a society that cannot bring life into the world.

The war plays of Euripides underscore this reality and hauntingly so. But there is yet something profound and healing in these war plays: pity. Pity is the great pathological feeling that Euripides's plays rouse. The shocking and scandalous imagery that Euripides uses prompts his audience to pity the victims of wanton sacrifice, cruelty, and butchery. Pity offers a way out of that society enslaved by hatred and war.

This essay was first published by *The Imaginative Conservative*, 3 February 2021.

Chapter 6

Aristophanes: The First Poet Critic

Aristophanes is the greatest of the classical comedians. His surviving plays are considered the high-water mark of ancient comedy and are filled with sensualism, blasphemy, and ridicule. Aristophanes, as Leo Strauss aptly said of him, was a reactionary. But he was also a modernist. In fact, reaction and modernity often occur together. Moreover, Aristophanes was the first outright social and literary critic the Western world ever produced—his plays being elongated, if not all so subtle, commentaries on Greek society, contemporary events, and literature.

Aristophanes's Life and Epoch

While the playwrights prior to Aristophanes lived in exciting and transformative times, Aristophanes's career spanned the apogee of Athenian power and degeneracy. His early years coincided with the turbulence of war and tyranny. And by the time of his death, formal philosophy was taking shape, with the rise of Socrates and Plato. In some sense, Aristophanes also lived through turbulent times. Although satirized by Plato in the *Symposium*, Aristophanes was friends with Socrates, and he was respected by Socrates and Plato. Aristophanes, like Socrates (and Plato) was an opponent of the demagogues and sophists; however, Aristophanes was also a stalwart defender of the necessity of poetry and mythology.

While Sophocles and Euripides also lived through the turbulence of the Peloponnesian War and the fall of Athenian democracy, Aristophanes was too young to remember the glory days of Athens, and his formative years took place under the tyranny of Cleon, the trials and tribulations of war, and the defeat of Athens by the Peloponnesian coalition. It was in the sorrow and sad trials of war that Aristophanes's comedy, social and political criticism, was born. Part of Aristophanes's literary efforts, then, were aimed at understanding how Athens had fallen into conflict and dissolution.

The First Political Critic (*Wasps*)

Aristophanes's comedy, the *Wasps*, is the first extensive and thorough work of political (and social) criticism in the Western literary tradition. It is also a battle of the generations, but it ends not how one would expect it. The two main characters are also linked to the tyrant Cleon, an Athenian general who ascended to popular acclaim in defeating Sparta at the Battle of Sphacteria (425 B.C.) and became the first leader of Athens from the ascendant commercial class. Philocleon, whose name literally means lover of Cleon, comes into conflict with his son, Bdelycleon, whose name in Greek means hater of Cleon.

During the opening moments of the play, we are made to sympathize with Philocleon because his son ridicules him as insane and describes him as akin to a rodent: "My father's got into the kitchen and he's scurrying about like a rat. Keep an eye on the waste pipe, and see that he doesn't get out that way." In describing his father as a rodent, Bdelycleon is set up—intentionally—by Aristophanes as the radical, but he will later reverse this image and show Philocleon to be the radical and Bdelycleon as the pious and patriotic son (thus subverting the traditional imagery and notion of the older generation being traditional and family-oriented while the younger generation is loose in morals and simply concerned with material pleasure and prestige).

Although Athens was still a democracy during Cleon's rule, Aristophanes penetrates the veil of political propaganda and asserts that Cleonic Athens was, in fact, tyrannical. It was tyrannical because it had become dominated by the politics of wealth and pleasure. It was tyrannical because the family had been destroyed and the demagogic state had swept into the vacuum. Cleonic Athens was tyrannical because of the collapse of filial piety and the domination of politics and human-to-human relationships by wealth and the pursuit of pleasure.

Showing his astute political skill, Aristophanes, through the speeches, criticizes the Athenian imperium. During the infamous trial scene between son and father, Bdelycleon critiques Philocleon's worldview and practices; they are practices that produce degeneracy and weakness rather than power. Furthermore, through the speech of Bdelycleon, Aristophanes attacks the commercial way of political life: "[N]ow tell me what advantages you gain from your dominion over all Greece?" he asks his father. Philocleon responds by saying, "Well, for one thing we see all the boys in the nude when they come up for inspection." Here, Aristophanes links wealth and power with licentious lust and pederasty, the latter of which had become a dominant practice among the wealthy elite in Athens in the late fifth century B.C.. This is no truly happy way to live, as Aristophanes will come to assert later. In fact, it leads to the destruction of filial warmth and the cornerstone of the polis.

In critiquing what has become of the Athenian political system, Bdelycleon says, "The people you elect to rule over you, because you're taken in by their speeches. And on top of that there are bribes they get from subject cities: three hundred thousand drachmas at a time, extorted by threats and intimidation." Aristophanes is critiquing the Athenian practice of extortionist imperialism through and through. No one can miss the obvious (hence why Cleon hated Aristophanes and the two came into conflict regularly before Cleon's death).

The critical speech given by Bdelycleon contrasts so substantially from the speech of the Athenian delegates in Thucydides's *History of the Peloponnesian War*, who assert, "We did not gain this empire by force. It came to us at a time when you were unwilling to fight on to the end against the Persians," and, "At this time our allies came to us on their own accord and begged us to lead them." While Thucydides wrote after Aristophanes, the mentality of the Athenian delegates presented by Thucydides was the mentality of the Athenian exceptionalism that Aristophanes skewered and undressed in the *Wasps*.

Once we accept the reality that Aristophanes was undertaking a heroic attempt at political criticism never before seen in Western literature, we can come to appreciate his great insight that when tyranny is threatened it lashes out at its critics with charges of conspiracy and tyranny in return. When Bdelycleon threatens the pleasurable and licentious life of his father, the chorus boldly (and ridiculously) proclaims, "Treason and treachery! Now it is clear! Tyranny, as ever, strikes from the rear." (Do note the comedic construction from Aristophanes's genius.) Bdelycleon responds, "It's always 'tyranny' and 'conspiracy' with you people, isn't it?"

After all, the setting of the *Wasps* is in court, a trial, but it is not Bdelycleon and Philocleon that are on trial; it is Athens herself on trial through the dazzling criticism of Aristophanes who is interrogating it.

In the first act of the *Wasps*, Aristophanes engages in some of the most robust and scandalous political criticism which remained unrivaled until St. Augustine's deconstruction of Rome in the *City of God*. Aristophanes accuses his native Athens of engaging in extortionist imperial politics. He asserts that the licentious and pederastic way of life developing in Athens weakens her and makes her a slave instead of being strong and free. He also mocks the Athenian justice system as being unconcerned with innocence and justice. He also suggests and that sophistic speeches and money (i.e. bribery and corruption) are the only things that matter to judge and jury. After all, the setting of the *Wasps* is in court, a trial, but it is not Bdelycleon and Philocleon that are on trial; it is Athens herself on trial through the dazzling criticism of Aristophanes who is interrogating it as previously mentioned.

The conclusion of the *Wasps* is equally shocking. Philocleon is seen pleasuring himself with a slave girl. Bdelycleon frees her from his father's lustful grip. Philocleon slaps Bdelycleon across the face in return. But the two eventually reconcile, and Philocleon comes to see the errors of his ways.

In an image that is reminiscent of the greatest image of filial piety in the ancient world—Aeneas carrying his father out of the burning ashes of Troy (a story the Greeks knew and wasn't invented by Virgil)—Bdelycleon carries his father indoors for his own safety and benefit. That image reveals Bdelycleon to be the defender of the old virtues and not his father. The chorus sings in rapturous applause, "At last he has fallen on happier days…His son, as all right-thinking men will agree, has shown both good sense and devotion; His kindness and charm are so touching to see that I'm quite overcome with emotion…The success that he's had in defending his father is a mark of his filial affection."

In offering political criticism, Aristophanes shows us the way forward, ironically, by going backward. To escape the lustful grip of tyranny, conspiracy, and slavery, we must return to filial affection and the resuscitation of the family. This is patently clear given that the chaos of most of the play pits a father against a son—in other words: family against family. At the same time, the decadence and degeneracy of Athens was brought forth by the commercial interests and way of life embodied by Cleon, who is instantiated in the play as Philocleon, and one could maintain that Aristophanes inserted himself into the play as Bdelycleon. Aristophanes did pay a great price in accosting Cleon during his reign over Athens. Aristophanes was denounced by Cleon and his critical plays dealing with Cleon did not win the awards that he would later win after Cleon's death.

The Birth Pangs of Literary Criticism (*Frogs*)

Beyond political criticism, Aristophanes also engaged in the first primitive iteration of literary criticism. While literary criticism, as a modern discipline and enterprise, began with Alexander Pope's critical translation and assessment of Homer's *Iliad*, Aristophanes was engaged in literary analysis in his own works—especially in his famous play the *Frogs*.

Though a reactionary in values, Aristophanes was also a modernist when it came to style. Aristophanes did not envision a return to the older agrarian Athens. Nor was his poetry owed to Hesiod, Homer, or Aeschylus. "The poet" whom Aristophanes was indebted to was Euripides. In fact, all of his plays make substantial homages to Euripides, and Euripides is even a central character in several of his plays. Aristophanes's literary style was Euripidean. But Aristophanes lampooned his literary master, exposing him, in the process, of being far beneath Aeschylus and Sophocles.

This is what makes the *Frogs* so shocking in its conclusion. Dionysus descends into the underworld to resurrect Euripides because there are no good poets anymore. Dionysus stumbles through the underworld and makes mistake after mistake and is bailed out by his slave, Xanthias, while constantly making reference to Euripides in the process. But when Dionysus finally reaches Euripides, he beholds a conflict between Aeschylus and his favorite poet. Dionysus sits to serve as a judge over who is the greater poet.

Up to this point, the *Frogs* has been filled with many references and allusions of Euripides which gives the audience a false sense of pro-Euripidean security. As mentioned, he is referred to as "the poet" in the play. Dionysus loves him. As he should. Euripides's play the *Bacchae* features Dionysus as a central figure (though Euripides presents Dionysus as a hollow and bloodthirsty god though Dionysus probably didn't care much for the truthful depiction). When Dionysus judges in favor of Aeschylus and resurrects him to save Athens, Aristophanes is expecting us to know— beyond the literary merits of Aeschylus—what the great poet-playwright advocated.

Aeschylus, as we know, was the great poet of Athena, of love, reason, and justice. In the penultimate showdown between the two dramatic tragedians, Euripides simply blurts out a rhetorically florid answer, "Believe the unsure safe, the safe unsure, mistrust what you now trust, and fear no more." Given Aristophanes's loathing of the sophists, he is also esoterically asserting that Euripides was a sophist.

After Euripides's answer, Dionysus is confused and asks for clarification—a moment that indicates the sophistic language employed by

Euripides. Euripides reformulates his answer in a twofold response. Thus, Euripides answered three times to say the same thing.

When Dionysus approached Aeschylus, the poet disciple of Athena first asks by inquiring into the situation that Athens now finds herself, "Tell me, what kind of people is the city electing these days? Honest, noble sorts?" Dionysus answers, "Where have you been? She hates them most of all!" Aeschylus converses with Dionysus by rhetorically asking, "She prefers hypocrites and swindlers?" Dionysus answers, "She doesn't prefer them, but she has no choice." Aeschylus closes by saying, "Well, if the city doesn't know its own mind, I don't see how it can be saved."

Euripides—like the libertarian sophist he is—does not engage in critical inquiry or conversation. He just talks. Aeschylus, being the disciple of reason and justice, inquires and converses with Dionysus—as an embodied participant of logos—before giving his response. Aeschylus's response employs reason, conversation, and inquiry—the very things necessary for civilization to flourish. The chorus ends by singing, "Fortunate is the man who has a mind with sharp with intelligence." Tradition and experience trump youth and passionate vigor; Aeschylus was the man of tradition and experience while Euripides, though dead, was the embodiment of youthful impetuousness. Aeschylus is subsequently resurrected to "save the city for us" for "[e]ducat[ing] the fools." Here, Aristophanes harshly mocks Athenian exceptionalism yet again by presenting Athens as a den of fools preferring hypocrites and swindlers rather than honest and noble leaders.

Aristophanes not only adjudicates in favor of the literary merits of Aeschylus; he also adjudicates for the traditional wisdom, filial piety, and rationalism of Aeschylus over the passionate vigor of Euripides, even if the literary and social modernity wrought by Euripides is very much the literary river in which Aristophanes swam. As such, Aristophanes sees the greatness of Aeschylus as not simply having been literary but also societal and practical. After all, he allows Aeschylus to say, "the truly great artist has always had a useful lesson to teach."

Sex, Violence, and the Critique of Empire

Lysistrata is, in my opinion, the greatest of the surviving plays by Aristophanes. Modern feminist readings are crude and have been roundly criticized by classicists; the proto-feminist readings miss the weight and scope of Aristophanes's through-going reactionary outlooks that Leo Strauss examined in *Socrates and Aristophanes*. *Lysistrata* is not the culminating work of his so-called "peace plays." Instead, it is Aristophanes's most daunting and profound work of civilizational criticism. It is his most mature and intellectual work, along with being his most risqué and shocking work.

Lysistrata is Aristophanes's attempt to fully wrestle with sexual deviancy, tyranny, and war. The play is filled, from start to finish, with sexual innuendo after sexual innuendo. Given the later date of *Lysistrata* in comparison to the *Wasps*, which also—though more subtly—dealt with sexual deviancy and degeneracy, *Lysistrata* is Aristophanes's attempt to fully wrestle with sexual deviancy, tyranny, and war (and how they are all interrelated in way that would make Camille Paglia blush). The first three gods invoked in the play, Bacchus, Aphrodite, and Pan, are all nymphomaniacs. When Lysistrata begins explaining her "very big plan," Calonice playfully responds, *món kaí pachý* (do you mean something long and thick?). Lysistrata answers with a counter pun, *kaí ní Día pachý* (indeed, something very long and thick).

Lysistrata's big plan is fully revealed when she says, "We must renounce – sex." The women around her are disturbed by the plan. They begin to cry and walk away until Lysistrata convinces them to stay. Even after several days of success, the solidarity of the women is tested when various women make excuses to get away and have sex.

That the women are so disturbed by the need to renounce sex in favor of chastity or virginity testifies to the sexual violence of Athens during the final decades of the fifth century B.C.. (Something that Euripides deftly deals with in his plays, especially the *Bacchae*, *Medea*, and the *Trojan Women*). It is, therefore, significant that Lampito, the Spartan woman of the play, is the first to agree with Lysistrata. The unity of Lysistrata and Lampito, of Sparta and Athens, also mocks the notion of Athenian exceptionalism yet again. In fact, it takes a Spartan to help bring about the peace that all will benefit from.

Over the course of the play, however, Aristophanes assails the older depiction of women as nymphomaniacs. But that doesn't mean he was a proto-feminist as some modern readings try to extrapolate—or that the women of the play are sexually modest. They most certainly are not as Lysistrata tells her sisters in arm to dress provocatively and to entice men as far as possible without succumbing to the sexual act like a "lioness-on-a-cheesegrater"; the women of the play must learn sexual modesty and control over the course of the play and devote themselves to the goddess Athena instead of Bacchus, Pan, or Aphrodite.

Nearly half-way through the play, Aristophanes reveals the most important speech by Lysistrata when she is confronting the chauvinistic and warlike Magistrate. When the Magistrate barks, "What have you ever done for the war effort?," Lysistrata answers with the cold truth that the future of civilization rests on the family and that the burden of civilization falls on women, not men:

> We've contributed to it twice over and more. For one thing, we've given you sons, and then had to send them off to fight…For another, we're in the prime of our lives, and how can we enjoy it, with our husbands always away on campaign and us left at home like widows? And quite apart from us married women, what about the unmarried ones who are slowly turning into old maids…A man comes home – he may be old and grey – but he can get himself a young wife in no time. But a woman's not in bloom for long, and if she isn't taken quickly she won't be taken at all, and before long she's left sitting at home hoping to see some omen foretelling a happier future.

Lysistrata is a play extolling and promoting the virtue of virginity and chastity despite the sexually charged and imagistic language surrounding it. After all, the gods Bacchus, Aphrodite, and Pan are superseded by the virgin queen Artemis and the virgin goddess Athena. (In doing so, Aristophanes nods in agreement with Aeschylus that Athena is the supreme goddess.) The reconciling image at the conclusion of the play is of men and women, husband and wife, united together in joyful song and feast. The participants sing a song to Athena to celebrate peace and the restoration of family. The peace won by women was through their learning of chastity and men also learning to control their lust to dominate.

Aristophanes simultaneously deconstructs the nymphomaniac image of women that had come to dominate Athenian consciousness by showing them to be ones who can control their sexual desires, while depicting the men as sexually depraved animals some 2,400 years before Sigmund Freud. Women set the bar for civilization and control the course of civilization because they bear the burden of child-rearing and labor. However, Aristophanes also maintains, as Lysistrata's culminating speech indicates, that women are happy as wives and mothers. The joyful life for a woman is to live the married life with a faithful husband and children in peace and not in isolation as a widow or, heaven forbid, unwed where they sulk away in isolation and rage leading them to kill their husbands and children like Clytemnestra or Medea. Moreover, the women of the play metaphorically represent the primacy of the household; the men, by contrast, represent the lust to dominate and the tyranny of Athens. It is women, not men, who are the heart and head of the family according to Aristophanes.

Beneath *Lysistrata*, Aristophanes is also engaged in a long-running commentary on the relationship of sex, violence, and war. Augustine may have summarized it better and more explicitly, but we can see in the play (and through much of Aristophanes's surviving corpus) how sexual lust leads to the *libido dominandi*—the lust to dominate. Athens was guilty of provoking the war with Sparta precisely because it couldn't control its appetites in more ways than one.

Thucydides reveals that it was always the goal of Athens to consummate an empire from the coasts of Ionia, down to Libya, Sicily, and even Carthage. As Euripides began to reveal in his plays and as Aristophanes makes explicit in his, the sex-craved festivals, nymphomaniac gods, and the indulgence of sexual gratification and sexual slavery that had gripped Athens coincided with Athens's lust for empire leading to the destruction of family, the imposition of tyranny, and, ultimately, the fall of Athens. There was, in Aristophanes's mind, a direct connection between the inability to control the sexual passions with the sudden explosion of political and military violence which was thrust upon Greece by Athens.

Lysistrata is a profound play worthy of psychological and sociological consideration, even if we may not necessarily agree with Aristophanes's "reactionary" answer to the problem of sex, violence, and imperialism (or even agree that sexual deviancy leads to societal and political violence).

The Genius of Aristophanes

That Aristophanes is one of the few poets who Plato includes in his dialogues also reveals the respect Plato had for Athens' great poetic genius. As I've written before concerning Plato's inclusion of Aristophanes in the *Symposium*, "Plato, through Socrates, is decidedly on the side of the poets. He is not only engaged in a re-mythology against the de-mythologizers, but he also draws on the two partial truths revealed by the mad Aristophanes and the eloquent Agathon, synthesizing the two together in Socrates's most remarkable dialogue and vision which has reverberated through the millennia." Prior to the rise of the post-Socratic tradition of philosophy the true wellspring of Greek intellectual thought was not in the sophists or even the pre-Socratics, but in the poets.

However, the supersession of poetry by philosophy revealed the eventual insufficiency of poetry to wrestle with the crises that beset Greek civilization in the fifth and fourth centuries. Greek literature dealt with what Giambattista Vico called sublime metaphysics, or poetic metaphysics. More specifically, the course of Greek literature deals with pathos. From Hesiod and Homer down through the playwrights, we see the cosmos moved by emotion and passion. While some of the pre-Socratic philosophers challenged this view, it wasn't until the rise of Plato that the insufficiency of the pathological cosmos was superseded by the rational cosmos.

Nevertheless, among the Greek poets and playwrights, Aristophanes deserves the greatest amount of our time and consideration. Aristophanes showed how poetry can be intensely intellectual and profound. He tried, in his fight against Socrates, to preserve poetry as a rival to emergent philosophy as an intellectual enterprise worthy of our respect. If "the truly great artist has always had a useful lesson to teach," then Aristophanes left us much to consider.

This essay was first published by *Merion West*, 4 September 2019.

Chapter 7

Herodotus and the Quest for Justice

Herodotus of Halicarnassus is the most famous historian of antiquity. He is also the patron saint of journalist-historians, that rare breed of men and women of the pen who relate exciting tales from afar in a prose digestible and energetic to read. Is there a theme that unites the seemingly disparate and elongated work of *The Histories*? What drives *The Histories* onward? Herodotus certainly did not have a conception of History as we moderns tend to have, but Herodotus's *Histories* does have a major theme underlying its composition—the contest between justice and injustice, or, properly, between *tisis* and *hybris*, and how this governs human action.

It is false to suggest that Herodotus is the historian of social justice. But it is true to say that Herodotus gives a lot of consideration to the problem of justice and how the desire for justice governs human action. As Donald Lateiner wrote long ago, "Herodotus's extension of *tisis* from a merely ethical principle to an encompassing law of nature is now widely recognized."

At face value, *The Histories* is the account of the war between the Greeks and the Persians, which ended in the defeat of the supposedly monstrous and barbarous Persian Empire at the hand of a collection of rough Greek city-states who even had conspirators in their midst (a sad fact that the city-states that allied with the Persians would never be allowed to forget). Yet a deeper reading of *The Histories* shows an intensely philosophical and inquisitive man that is sometimes lost in the long digressions on ethnography and cultural practices of diverse peoples. Herodotus was, and remains, however, a deep thinker of the highest caliber despite popular—if not otherwise ignorant— ridicule of him as a mythmaker and liar.

History, as we know, comes from the Greek word *historia*. The problem with history for moderns is that we have inherited two rather recent conceptions of history born of the Enlightenment mode of thinking. Many will no doubt be familiar with the notion of "scientific history" best encapsulated by Leopold von Ranke's conception of *wie es eigentlich gewesen*. The other conception of history is born out of modern philosophy; Hegel is probably the most notable figure in the crafting of Historicism, but the Progressive or Whig view of History is what most moderns will immediately recognize: the belief that history progresses from darkness and primitivism to light and civility over a period of organic successions. Both conceptions of history were alien to the Greeks and therefore unknown to Herodotus. Reading Herodotus (or Thucydides, for that matter) as a "scientific historian" misses the point; it also does tremendous harm in understanding the point of the work.

Historia, in Greek, means inquiry. What, then, is Herodotus inquiring into? "Herodotus of Halicarnassus here displays his inquiry, so that human achievements may not become forgotten in time, and great and marvelous deeds—some displayed by Greeks, some by barbarians—may not be without their glory; and especially to show why the two peoples fought with each other."

In his opening, Herodotus evokes Homer and states the reality of his work being an inquiry into human action. Herodotus does not invoke the muses, as Homer does. However, like Homer, human beings are the subject of his inquiry. Herodotus is more the heir of Homer than it initially seems.

Homer, moderns crudely believe, wrote a poetic fairy-tale. Or at least some people still believe this. It was common through much of the nineteenth century to believe the Trojan War to be poetic invention—until the discovery of a burnt-out city on the coast of Turkey gave greater credence to the view that the Trojan War had some basis in reality. We must remember, however, that Homer—though a poet—sung of a man, Achilles. Homer, as I have written before, begins the humanistic turning in Western consciousness. Hesiod's *Theogony* sung the praises of bloodthirsty and capricious gods; Homer's poems—while still retaining the gods as central figures—focus on men. Moreover, Homer's epics are adventures marked by war and conflict; the astute reader of Herodotus will immediately recognize, now, that he is indeed the heir of Homer. Herodotus, after all, is chiefly concerned with "human achievements" so that they will "not become forgotten in time" and writes a work that is an adventure narrative across many landscapes and cities dominated by the maelstrom of war and conflict. Herodotus's own prose and style, for those who can read Greek, mirrors that of Homer.

The first book of *The Histories* paints for us the picture of a bleak world not far removed from the dark agonistic cosmos of Hesiod. Herodotus's inquiry begins by telling stories of abduction and rape, acts of injustice which get the ball rolling, "These women were standing about near the vessel's stern, buying what they fancied, when suddenly the Phoenician sailors passed the word along and made a rush at them. The greater number got away; but Io and some others were caught and bundled aboard the ship, which cleared at once and made off for Egypt." As Herodotus goes on tell, "This, according to the Persian account, was how Io came to Egypt; and this was the first in a series of unjust acts." The Greeks subsequently land in Tyre and repay the Phoenicians back for their unjust act by abducting Europa and bringing her back to Hellas, thus bestowing the continental name to Europe.

In the opening moments of *The Histories*, Herodotus informs us that injustice is what propels the narrative forward—and how unjust acts lead to a desire for justice. Aristotle may have provided the most familiar account of justice in the Greek world, paying each his due, but the Greek understanding of justice was essentially punitive and retributive. τίσις, or *tisis*, is the Greek word for justice which Herodotus uses in his work; and *tisis* is entirely retributive in its Greek context and understanding. As Hipparchus later learns from the oracle, "No man does wrong and shall not the penalty bear." There would be no great movement of human action without the motivating impulse of justice to punish a preceding act of injustice. At the start, then, Herodotus lets us know there is something deep about his inquiry: it is an inquiry into human action and how justice, *tisis*, is at the core of the human condition which is shared by Greeks and "barbarians" alike.

The first book seems far removed from the Persian Wars which occurred in the fifth century B.C., but with the understanding that Herodotus is investigating human action—and principally the role of justice as a governing force for human action—we can begin to understand the remoteness and obscurity of the many stories before we finally arrive at the climax of human action up to Herodotus's time: the battle for justice that was the Persian Wars.

After discussing the abduction and rape of Io and Europa, Herodotus tells us the story of the abduction of Helen by Paris of Troy and the Trojan War which followed and ended with the sack and burning of Troy, "Such then is the Persian story. In their view it was the capture of Troy that first made them enemies of the Greeks." Herodotus, though a Greek partisan, does give consideration to "the Persian story" and explains why the Persians felt themselves in the right in seeking to conquer Greece: the Greeks had first conquered a brother of the east.

From there, Herodotus proceeds to tell us what many might regard as mythic stories of courtly rape and usurpation. Again, to get lost in the supposed fictionality of these stories—for that is what "myth" means in Greek—is to again miss the point of Herodotus's inquiry. These stories, brutal and banal as they sometimes are, all underscore the reality of revenge, power, justice, and injustice which govern human action and advances the inquiry ("history") further. We also witness an investigation of human psychology over committing unjust acts like when Gyges usurped the throne and then sought out the Delphi Oracle to have a story legitimize his seizure of power. Knowing one has committed injustice leads to a pervasive psychological guilt—a guilt which St. Augustine would further develop in his psychology of sin and Original Guilt—but that guilt can be assuaged if divine sanction backs it up.

This accruement of mass power is what is called *hybris*, or immense pride, which is necessarily culled by an act of destruction which the Greeks called *nemesis*.

In relaying the long story of Croesus, who is important because he came into conflict with King Cyrus of Persia in the prelude to the Persian Wars, after hearing the news of the death of his son in a hunting accident "Croesus prayed to Zeus…to witness what he had suffered at the hands of his guest; he invoked [Zeus] again under his title of Protector of the Hearth, because he had unwittingly entertained his son's murderer in his own house; and yet again as God of Guest-Friendship, because the man he had sent to guard his son had turned out to be his bitterest enemy." In the story of Croesus, we witness the long march and desire, nay, demand, for justice which becomes the retributive fuel that advances human action to seek closure.

The "great and marvelous deeds" of men that Herodotus wants to eulogize are actions seeking justice against injustice. Caught up in this turbulent struggle is how pride cometh before the fall; for Herodotus, power is the product of injustices piled upon injustices—as should be clear after reading the first book. Power is constantly usurped by acts of betrayal, treachery, and murder. The attainment of power subsequently inflates the ego in a conceit of self-importance. This accruement of mass power is what is called *hybris*, or immense pride, which is necessarily culled by an act of destruction which the Greeks called *nemesis*.

The Persians may have felt themselves justified in their war against the Greeks by reaching back to the past and invoking the destruction of Troy as their *casus belli* for war, but here Herodotus's pro-Greek sentiments begin to show. "The Persians, whom Darius had left in Europe under Megabazus' command, began hostilities against the Greeks on the Hellespont by subduing the Perinthians, who refused to accept Persian domination." Herodotus, in resuming the narrative of the Persian War at long last, informs us that the Perinthians refused to be subjugated to Persian imperialism. Importantly, the Persians are also "in Europe" having transgressed the natural boundary of Europe and Asia, which is the Hellespont.

Persia is no longer the small but consolidated kingdom it was prior to the sacking of Babylon. It has grown into an oversized empire filled with *hybris* over its glorious conquests and accomplishments. Everywhere the Persians go, Herodotus tells us, they commit injustices. Forced relocation, slavery, and subjugation are just a few of the injustices they commit as their power expands by these acts of injustice. When enslaving the men and women of Lemnos, Herodotus explains, "The reason Otanes gave for subjugating and enslaving all these people was that some had shirked service in the Scythian expedition, while others had molested Darius' army on its way home."

While Herodotus does portray the Persians as despotic and unjust, he is remarkably even-handed all things considered. Just as he had—all the way back in the first book—informed us that the Persians invoked the destruction of Troy as their call for justice against Greek invasion and colonization, even here—in more nakedly brutal episodes—"the Persian story" is interwoven into the narrative. The Persians felt injustice done unto them at earlier times; this was merely the manifestation of justice repaying a prior act of injustice. So, while we know that Herodotus felt the Greeks were in the right to seek justice against Persian aggression, whenever we look carefully at his narrative, he does give the Persian side of the story.

Herodotus, as we can begin to see, is a theorist of human action—and a theorist of justice. Justice, according to Herodotus, is the chief force of human action. Justice—his inquiry is clearly telling us—is what governs all human action. Fathers, sons, warriors, kings, queens, priests and priestesses all cry out to their gods for justice (retributive justice) to be done. Again, Herodotus is not far removed from Homer in this regard; for Homer repeatedly has his characters cry out to Zeus and the other gods for justice after having been spited by an act of injustice. (Though Homer has a more subtle deconstruction of the injustice of the gods in mind when he does so—for the gods never do come procure justice for their devotees in *The Iliad*.) It is now clear why Herodotus juxtaposes "the Persian story" with "the Greek account" in this dialectical tale of contrasts; he wishes us to think alongside him about the nature of justice. Is the Persian account of justice truly just? We obviously know what Herodotus thought, but he never denies the Persian side of the story, even if we are meant to view "the Persian story" as manifestly unjust.

What brings the Greeks and Persians into full blown war are acts of injustice demanding acts of retributive justice in return. Aristagoras of Miletus sails to Hellas to try and convene an alliance of Greek city-states to help their beleaguered brethren in Asia Minor. Rebuffed, initially, by Sparta, Aristagoras makes progress in Athens. Herodotus again gives a extensive digressive backstory, but it is still filled with themes of power, usurpation, justice and injustice.

Aristagoras convinces the Athenians to aid them in their struggle against Persian expansionism. Greek custom and history now comes into conflict with Persian expansionist power. Aristagoras has been, thus far, an ambassador seeking justice and liberty on behalf of those suffering injustice and oppression (this makes Aristagoras's fate even more tragic since he becomes the very thing he fretted, a despotic conqueror). Now, in Athens' entry into this abyss of violence and revenge the themes of liberty and justice against despotism and injustice come to the fore.

While it is seductive to see the tale of liberty and despotism pervading *The Histories* it should be clear, upon closer inspection, that this theme which had been catapulted to the front of our readings of Herodotus by the Whigs is actually secondary to the larger theme of justice and injustice that guides the entire work. Liberty, to be sure, manifests on the side of justice just as despotism manifests on the side of injustice but the liberty-despotism dialectic is a product of the modern conceptions of history otherwise alien to Herodotus and his contemporaries. Take, for example, the great poet-playwright Aeschylus.

Aeschylus had served with the Athenians at Marathon and likely served at the Battle of Salamis. Undoubtedly Athenian in orientation, even his play *The Persians* doesn't put liberty vs. tyranny as the central concern of the play. Instead, it is the illusive question of justice which pervades the play (as it does in *The Oresteia*.) Liberty, life, and love when it does manifest in the Greek literary corpus is always subordinate to quest for justice. The Greeks lose liberty, life, and love whenever injustice rears its ugly head.

Returning to the Athenian intervention, the Athenians burn the Cybebe Temple of Sardis down—a city and temple now under the control of the Persians. "In the conflagration at Sardis a temple of Cybebe, a goddess worshiped by the natives," Herodotus writes, "was destroyed, and the Persians later made this a pretext for their burning of Greek temples." Again, even here the Persian side of the story is recounted. We witness an act of injustice (from the Persian perspective) which motivates them to take revenge (retributive justice) against the Athenians. "The story goes," Herodotus relays to us when considering the emotional outburst of Darius, "that when Darius learned of the disaster, he did not give a thought to the Ionians, knowing perfectly well that the punishment for their revolt would come; but he asked who the Athenians were, and then, on being told, called for his bow. He took it, set an arrow on the string, shot in up into the air and cried, 'Grant, O God, that I may punish the Athenians.'"

Herodotus helps to give thematic consideration to the Persian War by the end of the fifth book. Human nature, it is now clear, is moved by desire for (retributive) justice (*tisis*). But what is the basis for the breach of justice? The lack of honoring custom and natural boundaries. The Persians, as they expand, breach all the customary laws and traditions of the people they conquer. In conquering them they also expand beyond normal boundaries. This feeds them with *hybris*, powerful pride, which demands destruction at the hands of those seeking justice.

Justice and injustice, now, is the unmistakable spirit guiding Herodotus's inquiry. In the sixth book we witness Persian injustice and despotism wherever they advance: pillage, destruction, and enslavement occur on a massive scale. This is the prospect waiting the free city-states of Greece who, as Herodotus has informed us through those long digressive backstories, had thrown off the old tyrannies and their injustice to enjoy the relative justice and liberty they now have. (The long digressions thus serve to emphasis the just defense of Greek liberty; even here, however, we once more see how liberty is still subordinate to justice.) Individual and collective acts of injustice are met by *tisis* which brings *nemesis* to the guilty party. Individually, we see this with Cleomenes and Miltiades. Collectively, we witness this with the Persians at the ferocious Battle of Marathon—the ultimate act of justice which brings destruction to the unjustly powerful. This will, however, renew the cycle of violence and the need for retributive justice from the side of the Persians.

Thus the cycle is renewed "[w]hen the news of the battle of Marathon reached Darius." Darius is enraged at the news of this defeat. As we are told, "he was more than ever determined to make war on Greece." So the war continues. Acts of injustice occur. They are countered by acts of retributive justice ending in destruction, often in the form of battle, and the cycle repeats *ad infinitum* until we reach the battles of Salamis, Plataea, and Mycale, which throw off the Persian yoke from the besieged Greeks.

Although we descend into a cycle of injustice and justice, which is manifested through violence, the eighth and ninth books see the slow then rapid dissolution and retreat of the Persians from Europe. Mycale returns us to Asia Minor where the Persians are once again defeated and the Ionian coast seemingly freed from the unjust tyranny of the Persians.

Herodotus gives great weight to human choice and action despite accusations of a theologized history. Again, this seems to me to be the product of blind Whig historians who see too much invoking of gods. But even where the gods are invoked, they are invoked for purely human reasons. The desire for justice. The desire for justification. The desire for sanction and remission of guilt for the crime of usurpation or patricide.

The organic and natural succession of events that constitute "history" from the modern mentality can be synthesized with Herodotus's account of human action governed by a dialectic of injustice and justice.

Moreover, human action in Herodotus is the result of human encounters. Whether the *femme fatale*, the treacherous murder, or the marauding invading army human action is undertaken not from face-to-face encounters with the divine but with mortal humans plagued by all the imperfections of human nature. Herodotus is, on this account, a very "modern" writer.

Can Herodotus be salvaged from the modernist disposition? If we take the minimalist approach to Historicism he most certainly can. The organic and natural succession of events that constitute "history" from the modern mentality can be synthesized with Herodotus's account of human action governed by a dialectic of injustice and justice. As *The Histories* open, an act of human injustice is counteracted by an act of retribution—what the Greeks would have considered justice. This starts the entire cycle of movement that takes from the seas and walls of Tyre, Troy, and Lydia, to Miletus, Athens, and Sparta. The manifold personalities we meet are also all too human in their desire and psychological problems. Augustine may have been the first systematic psychologist of the soul and will, but Herodotus anticipates the direction that Augustine will take by some 800 years.

Herodotus ought to have been required reading for the leaders, policy-wonks, and experts in the euphoria of the 1990's when the Soviet Union came tumbling down and the United States—leading the "free world"—embarked on imperial overreach and aggrandizement not that dissimilar from the Persians in Herodotus's *Histories*. Part of the fall of Persia was due to its extensive size and power. Persia is, by every account, far more powerful than the tiny city-states of Hellas who decided to stand up to her. The fall of Persia was preceded by a spirit of overweening power and pride that convinced her that she should—and could—rule the world. *Tisis*, then, is not only about retributive justice but also the hand that produces equipoise in an unbalanced world. Thus, we see why the final books bring us back to Asia Minor and the liberation of those formerly conquered Greek city-states.

The inquiry of Herodotus into the inner working of human action is what is most important for us today. The Whig view of history likes to claim we have made progressive strides away from our darker ghosts and base desires. Herodotus shows us that human action is governed by the desire for justice—especially after suffering an act of injustice (however just the justification may be). The whole movement of human action, as Herodotus's inquiry reveals, is the movement of justice confronting injustice. Yet, we also see—in Herodotus—how this desire for justice has a retributive and destructive side to it. We might remain unsure which side will win but the "great and marvelous deeds" which Herodotus sings of are the "great and marvelous deeds" of justice in a world filled with injustices. We are still the children of Herodotus after all.

This essay was first published by *Merion West*, 27 June 2020.

Chapter 8

The Moral Philosophy of Plutarch

Lucius Mestrius Plutarchus, better known as Plutarch, was the finest essayist of antiquity and the author of the famous and witty *Parallel Lives*. Plutarch was long an influential force in the development of Western humanities; a biographer, essayist, philosopher, and historian, his writings touched on all the subjects of the humanities from history and politics to philosophy and theology. The *Parallel Lives* might be his most famous work, but his collection of essays remembered to posterity as the *Moralia* is the most enduring.

Parallel Lives

Moralia is an appropriate name for Plutarch's essays. While not all of his essays are explicitly moral in orientation, nearly all of Plutarch's essays have moral instruction and guidance baked into them. This is also true when properly understanding the nature and purpose of the *Parallel Lives*. Plutarch was, first and foremost, a moralist. His reflections on great men, history, and politics are all subordinate to Plutarch's ambitious moral project which, in turn, was a byproduct of his Platonism.

Plutarch, like many of the new Platonists (Plutarch is generally considered belonging to the school of "Middle Platonism"), believed in an interconnected and relational cosmos. This is not necessarily surprising. The Platonist tradition in philosophy, Stoicism, and Christianity all conceived of a similar interconnected and enchanted cosmos. But this relational reality to Plutarch's philosophical and cosmic beliefs is undeniably visible in his many writings. The moral philosophy of Plutarch is never in isolation; it is on this account that Plutarch sharply broke with the Stoics and often criticized them (even if he was not fully aware of or charitable to their beliefs).

Parallel Lives is reflective of this interconnected world that Plutarch inhabited by the fact that he pairs the great men of his quasi-biographical history. The *Parallel Lives* is not simply a celebration of great men and their deeds in history; it is, in fact, a deconstruction of some great men and celebration of others. The contrasts that Plutarch constructs in his composition of the *Parallel Lives* is meant to allow "emulation and eagerness that may lead [the readers] on to imitation." But Plutarch does not explicitly tell us whom to emulate. We are meant to find that out for ourselves through our relational give-and-take with the great men of the *Parallel Lives*.

Let us look, for example, at two of the men Plutarch discusses: Pericles and Marcus Cato (Cato the Elder). These two men are not paired with each other; Pericles is paired with Fabius Maximus and Cato with Aristides. I have chosen to highlight Pericles and Cato because, in this examination of Pericles and Cato, we see the same contrasts that Plutarch sometimes constructs in his pairing of the great men throughout the book. I should add that the pairings do not necessarily stop with the two men contrasted with each other in the form Plutarch produced—all the men in the *Parallel Lives* are contrasted with each other, and this we should never forget.

Moral imitation and instruction are essential parts of Plutarch's philosophical project and the *Parallel Lives*. This is fully revealed when Plutarch writes, "Since, then, our souls are by nature possessed of great fondness for learning and fondness for seeing, it is surely reasonable to chide those who abuse this fondness on objects all unworthy either of their eyes or ears, to the neglect of those which are good and serviceable...Such objects are to be found in virtuous deeds; these implant in those who search them out a great and zealous eagerness which leads to imitation." Plutarch understands, or believes, that moral instruction and imitation go together. Imitation of virtuous souls is part of Plutarch's energetic writings.

The art of reading, as Plutarch knew, was itself a dialectic of encounter and engagement. The men whom he biographized do not stand alone. They are paired with another. That Plutarch wrote with a general reading audience in mind also reflects the dialectical and relational nature of reading and education. The art of reading, which is a moral enterprise for Plutarch, is being able to weed through the hazy maze of human action to find the good and bad and imitate only the good. This is why Plutarch contrasts good and bad men over the course of the *Parallel Lives*.

Plutarch's Case Studies: Men to Emulate, and Not

Pericles, for instance, is a man whom Plutarch so clearly admires and thinks is worthy of emulation:

"As a young man, Pericles was exceedingly reluctant to face the people, since it was thought that in feature he was like the tyrant Peisistratus; and when men well on in years remarked also that his voice was sweet, and his tongue glib and speedy in discourse, they were struck with amazement at the resemblance. Besides, since he was rich, of brilliant lineage, and had friends of the greatest influence, he feared that he might be ostracized, and so at first had naught to do with politics, but devoted himself rather to a military career, where he was brave and enterprising. However, when Aristides was dead, and Themistocles in banishment, and Cimon was kept by his campaigns for the most part abroad, then at last Pericles decided to devote himself to the people, espousing the cause of the poor and the many instead of the few and the rich, contrary to his own nature, which was anything but popular."

Upon the death of Pericles Plutarch writes, "So, then, the man is to be admired not only for his reasonableness and the gentleness which he maintained in the midst of many responsibilities and great enmities, but also for his loftiness of spirit, seeing that he regarded it as the noblest of all his titles to honor that he had never gratified his envy or his passion in the exercise of his vast power, nor treated any one of his foes as a foe incurable."

Marcus Cato, a well-known Roman and hero of the Republic, is a more sensitive subject. Having become a Roman citizen, Plutarch had to walk a fine line between praise and criticism of the heroic Roman pantheon. But when we read his reflections on Cato, we begin to see a subtle hand of criticism which suggests Cato is not a man entirely worthy of emulation.

Plutarch took his spiritual moralism to the point of vegetarianism and was, arguably, an early proponent of animal-rights. When talking about Cato Plutarch writes, "We see that kindness or humanity has a larger field than bare justice to exercise itself in; law and justice we cannot, in the nature of things, employ on others than men; but we may extend our goodness and charity even to irrational creatures; and such acts flow from a gentle nature, as water from an abundant spring." Here, we see how human morality is tied to the broader world in which we inhabit and exist in.

We have interconnected relationships with even the "irrational animals" that walk and run on four legs and depend on us for acts of compassion and kindness. In what becomes a moving and infuriating passage, Plutarch informs us about how Cato treated a noble horse he had reared from its youth: "Yet Cato for all this glories that he left that very horse in Spain which he used in the wars when he was consul, only because he would not put the public to the charge of his freight. Whether these acts are to be ascribed to the greatness or pettiness of his spirit, let every one argue as they please." Plutarch might qualify for us that we may argue as we please over the moral merits of Cato's action, but it is clear enough that Plutarch did not like Cato's decision to abandon his noble horse to die in Spain.

Yet, in the baseness of some men, there is also grandeur and goodness. As Plutarch says:

"[Cato] was also a good father, an excellent husband to his wife, and an extraordinary economist; and as he did not manage his affairs of this kind carelessly, and as things of little moment, I think I ought to record a little further whatever was commendable in him in these points. He married a wife more noble than rich; being of opinion that the rich and the high-born are equally haughty and proud; but that those of noble blood would be more ashamed of base things, and consequently more obedient to their husbands in all that was fit and right. A man who beat his wife or child laid violent hands, he said, on what was most sacred; and a good husband he reckoned worthy of more praise than a great senator; and he admired the ancient Socrates for nothing so much as for having lived a temperate and contented life with a wife who was a scold, and children who were half-witted."

We, in reading, must be able to determine the good from the bad and therefore not idolize men of renown without due criticism and reservation; some men might be worthy of outright emulation and imitation. Others are only worthy of some emulation and imitation, while realizing the bad that should be shunned and purged.

Moral Imitation and Progression

The importance of moral imitation and virtue is perhaps most explicitly seen in Plutarch's essay "On Being Aware of Moral Progress." The essay is a critique of Stoic moral philosophy which, at least as conceived of by Plutarch, leaves the individual in a state of limbo not knowing whether or not he or she is progressing in moral virtue. Plutarch seeks, in accord with his interconnected philosophy, a harmony of self with the world and a harmony of self with practical living.

Plutarch proceeds to offer a list and interpretation of signs which we can be assured indicate moral progression. Befitting the relation between Plutarch's cosmic vision and the importance he placed on friendship, one such sign is our ability to take criticism from friends who seek our growth and maturation. Warranted criticism, and being moved by it, is evidence of moral progression:

"Their own weakness, however, is not the only factor which can make students of philosophy waver and double back. The earnest advice of friends and the mocking, bantering attacks of critics, can also, on their occurrence, warp and sap resolve, and have been known to put some people off philosophy altogether. Therefore, a good indication of an individual's progress would be equanimity when faced with these factors, and not being upset or irritated by people who name his peers and tell him they are prospering at some royal household, or are marrying into money or are going down to the agora as the people's choice for some political or forensic post."

This matches with Plutarch's assessment that if we admit our faults and take criticism—warranted, to be sure—this is a definite sign of moral progress. Therefore, the man who insulates himself from any criticism and thinks himself superior is not progressing morally and reflects his own foolishness. As Plutarch writes, "The same goes for people with faults: it is the incurable ones who get angry and behave aggressively and fiercely towards anyone who tries to rebuke and reprimand them, whereas those who put up with rebuke and do not resist are in a more composed state." Given that Plutarch was writing in an age when reading and writing were elite and intellectual endeavors, this constitutes an esoteric critique aimed at stuffy and prideful intellectuals and wannabes who curse those who offer critiques and other views and, in their rage, reveal themselves to be petty and not worth listening to. If our so-called teachers, like the sophists in Plato's dialogues, fly into bestial rages at criticism, they reveal themselves to be frauds not worth emulating or learning from.

Imitation, moreover, is the ultimate manifestation of moral progression just as was explicitly stated in the *Parallel Lives*. When discussing the relationship and friendship of Miltiades and Themistocles, Plutarch writes that Themistocles "was also moved to emulate and imitate Miltiades. So we must regard our progress as minimal as long as our admiration of success lies fallow and remains inadequate in itself to spur us to imitation." If we cannot come to imitate the good and honest, the virtuous and wise, that speaks volumes of our own baseness and lack of moral progression. We must, as Plutarch writes, "love the character of those whose conduct we desire to imitate, and always to accompany our wanting to be like them with goodwill which awards them respect and honor. On the other hand, anyone feeling competitively envious of his betters must realize that it is jealousy of a certain reputation or ability that is provoking him, and that he is not respecting or admiring virtue."

Plutarch defends the view that we can know our moral progress—not to or never to be aware of our moral progress is self-defeating. Moral progress has a practical manifestation: how we live and act in life, especially in relations with others. Plutarch sees philosophy in the theoretical sense—as it was descending into during his time, especially as reflected by the Stoics—as problematic. We need to move beyond the self-absorption of mere theory to practical action and human living. This is the ultimate realization of moral progress: the imitation of good men and to live in harmony with friends and neighbors.

Anger and Harmony

"On the Avoidance of Anger," another one of Plutarch's influential essays, is odd in that it starts as a dialogue in the style of Plato but quickly descends into a monologue, with Fundanus becoming the sole speaker as the essay progresses. Yet the fact that this essay is a dialogue with two friends establishes the theme of relational friendship and the importation of wisdom from one friend to another, which are quintessential Plutarchan themes. For, as the dialogue-essay proceeds, one of the things we realize about the problem of anger is how it destroys one's relationship with the world and with friends.

The extreme passion of anger is a product of unreason, to be governed by anger is to be enslaved to passion. "It is best," Plutarch writes, "therefore, to keep calm, or alternatively to run away and hide and find refuge in silence, as though we realized that we were about to have a fit, and wanted to avoid falling, or rather falling on someone—and it is friends above all whom we must often fall on. We do not feel love or jealousy or fear for everyone but anger leaves nothing alone, nothing in peace: We get angry at enemies and friends, at children and parents, and even at gods and animals and inanimate objects."

Anger, as Plutarch deftly says, touches everything and can destroy everything—even those relationships that are most sacred and most cherished. (And let us not forget that certain figures in the *Parallel Lives*, like Pelopidas, are examples of how anger leads to destruction.)

Returning to imitation and virtue, Fundanus (who is the mouthpiece of Plutarch), says "I tried to understand anger by watching others." Moral imitation is—as should be clear by now—perhaps the greatest Plutarchan theme. Anger ruins the self and all relations the self has. Imitation of those who do not fly into rages of anger and destruction are the very persons whom we should imitate in our own avoidance of anger for the sake of harmony with the world and our friends. Even listening, as Plutarch explains in "On Listening," embodies this dialectical and imitative reality of moral progression and maturation.

Not only should we avoid anger, but we should also avoid excessive grief as well. In his most intimate and touching letter, "In Consolation to His Wife," Plutarch writes to Timoxena that they should be thankful for what was and what was not. Rather than dwell in the pit of despair and grief for not being able to see their only daughter grow up into adulthood and marriage, they should remember the joy that their infant daughter brought them before her passing. "No, our daughter," Plutarch reminds Timoxena, "was the sweetest thing in the world to hug and watch and listen to, and by the same token she must remain and live on in our thoughts."

Plutarch's philosophy of memory, as indicated here, is also not an insular or isolative reality (ore even activity). Memory, too, is related and attached to others and the world and has moral consequences for us. To remember in fondness brings stability and joy—to remember in grief and animosity brings revulsion and, eventually, anger. Affection, Plutarch reminds us in reminding his wife, is greater than grief. To fly away from grief to affection is just as much part of our moral pilgrimage as imitation of virtuous friends is. "Affection is what we gratify by missing, valuing, and remembering the dead, but the insatiable desire for grief—a desire which makes us wail and howl— is just as contemptible as hedonistic indulgence."

If grief entirely overwhelms us, we descend into a state of resentment and hatred, which is the pinnacle of darkness in Plutarch's philosophy: "You see, my dear, we will seem to regret that our child was ever born if we find more to complain about now than in the situation before her birth. We must not erase the intervening two years from our memories, but since they brought happiness and joy, we must count them as pleasant. The good was brief, but should not therefore be regarded as a long-term bad influence; and we should not be ungrateful for what we received just because our further hopes were dashed by fortune." By becoming miserable in our grief, we begin to hate ourselves and hate the world. In doing so we make everything around us miserable, too.

In a world often governed by passion, rage, and anger, Plutarch's moral philosophy and advocacy of harmony with others and the world stands out as a small but glistening light in the darkness. Those who complain about Plutarch's writings being tainted by his own voice, his own "ideological" program, completely miss the point of Plutarch's writings. Plutarch is not writing in the vein of Leopold von Ranke and the absurd notions of "history as it was." Plutarch sees the world of human action—which is encompassed in history—as a moral minefield that we must navigate in our ascent to moral perfection and harmony with the world.

This pilgrimage to find harmony in the world that exists is, in fact, deeply Platonic. It is erroneous to maintain that Plato's philosophy and the Platonic tradition advocated world flight. Plato's philosophy sought harmony in the world of nature because the world of nature reflected the ideal forms. The ideal forms, it is true, exist beyond our realm of nature but are accessible to us. In imitation of the ideal on earth, we become the ideal incarnate and instantiated. Because Plutarch's philosophy has a practical function (as did Plato's philosophy properly understood in its moral and political context), the practical manifestation of Plutarch's moral philosophy is the good and harmonious life in this world and not the next.

In reading Plutarch, we must seize the reins of the chariot of "ascent" and become noble souls who become lights in the world for others to emulate, imitate, and become friends with. Plutarch's philosophy is a grand revision of Plato's doctrine of the charioteer, with deep and profound implications for our lives and our world. Plutarch may have fallen on hard times recently because his vision of a harmonious world of moral relationships is the opposite of the so-called enlightened vision of a disconnected world of isolative individuals pursuing "hedonistic indulgence," but his vision of an interconnected and intimate life of moral purpose and friendship endures for eyes to see and ears to hear.

This essay was first published by *Merion West*, 18 February 2021.

Chapter 9

Plato's Symposium:
The Drama and Trial of Love

Plato's *Symposium* is one of the most iconic works of literature in the Western tradition. While *The Republic* may be more famous, the *Symposium* is the most graphic, intense, and dramatic of the dialogues. Its legacy has been far reaching, inspiring religion and mysticism, to visions of art, the good, and the beautiful. Plato's *Symposium* is about love, *eros* more specifically. But the dialogue, beyond being the culminating triumph of Plato's literary hand, is equally poetic. Plato stands on the side of the poets rather than the "philosophers." In fact, the dialogue is a mythological drama about the fate of love and its place in the new world born of technology, the political, and the philosophical.

Aristotle said that the lover of myth is also the lover of wisdom. The *Symposium* is unique among Plato's dialogue that two of the central speakers are poets, playwrights, the type of poets whom Plato wanted to ban in his ideal city in *The Republic*. Plato's harsh condemnation of the poets often causes us to fail to realize Plato was himself a poet. His works are dialogues. They incorporate myths. They tell grand tales of grandeur and fall. They are comedic and tragic. Plato may have been arrogant in thinking himself the true poet among imitators of the false image; yet, Plato's own artistry should be self-evident once given some thought. Plato's stories inspire us after two and half millennia while other philosophers, serious philosophers, who wrote equally serious tomes, have been forgotten to all except the specialists.

It is fitting that this dialogue on love includes a bunch of love triangles. Phaedrus, Pausanias, and Aristophanes form the trio of speakers who incorporate love with pederasty. Eryximachus, Agathon, and Socrates give speeches about how love pervades all things and form a trio in contrast to Phaedrus, Pausanias, and Aristophanes. We also have a trio embodying love as a judge; Alcibiades, Socrates, and Agathon all serve, in some capacity, as judges in the course of the dialogue. At the end of the dialogue, with night fallen, Socrates speaks with Aristophanes and Agathon.

The world of philosophy before Plato can be broken down into two epochs: the epoch of the Ionian metaphysicians and the age of the sophists. Plato was responding to both prior currents of philosophy in his many works. *Timaeus*, for instance, gives a famous cosmological account of the world and life that would have been more fitting to the bygone age of the Ionian metaphysicians; however, Plato rejects the atomism and hollow materialism of materialist and mechanical metaphysicians whose outlook would threaten to destroy *eros*. It isn't surprising, then, that one such speaker is included in the *Symposium* recapitulating this theme of materialist de- mythology. Plato's intense hatred for the sophists should be clear enough to anyone who has read Plato, and his emphasis on truth, ethics, and the good stand as the reactive force against the world of Thrasymachus, Glaucon, and Protagoras.

But the world before philosophy was the world of poetry and myth. That world, the garden of Hesiod, Homer, and Sappho, was threatened by the Ionian metaphysicians and sophists who saw no use in those silly and superstitious accounts of the gods, heroes, and captive souls. The birth of philosophy coincided with the birth of de-mythology; and the *Symposium* includes an intense struggle between the corrupt force of de-mythology and the life-giving and inspiration force of re-mythology. This contest between de-mythology and re-mythology, or mythology, is the drama of Eros.

Eros is on trial over the course of the *Symposium*. Eros, who is also a god, is therefore set in the crosshairs of those who claim to be defending him but are really destroying him. The trial of *eros* is also the trial of *physis*, of nature. The more central battle between de-mythology and mythology is also a crisis between *physis* and *nomos*, of nature and convention.

Symposium is also a political text as are all of Plato's dialogues. Even *Timaeus* is an esoteric account of the political. Socrates and Critias give political speeches and we fully expect Timaeus to do the same. Timaeus's lengthy discourse on cosmology, the Demiurge, mathematics, reason and necessity, eventually shows its hand toward the end when Timaeus says, "In addition, when men who are constitutionally unsound, as I've been describing, live in cities with pernicious political systems and hear correspondingly pernicious speeches… become bad" (*Timaeus*, 87b).

Plato is asking, without directly posing it, can the *polis* survive without *eros*? This equally entails, in relation to Aristophanes's iconoclastic speech, can the *polis* survive *eros* (at least as conceived by Aristophanes)? Must *eros* be destroyed for the *polis* to survive? Can *eros* be ordered to something productive and edifying rather than destructive and restless?

Culling Eros

The first person to speak in the *Symposium* is not one of the main speakers on *eros*. Instead, we have a flash-forward preface with Apollodorus and Glaucon. Glaucon is searching for Apollodorus to know how the famous speeches on love went. Plato's genius is seen even in the opening sentences of the dialogue. In searching for Apollodorus to know how the discourses on love went, Plato foreshadows what the dialogue is about: *eros* and knowledge. This brief introduction sets the stage for what is to come.

Phaedrus, Pausanias, and Eryximachus are the first principal characters to give their speeches on love. Pheadrus offers a brief account that amounts to love as selfishness; it is an internal desire not seeking anything outside of oneself. Phaedrus's account of love is premised on winning the affection of the other. Pausanias offers the next speech. Like Phaedrus, it is relatively short. Pausanias subjects *eros* to morality, specifically to friendship and law.

The two speeches by Phaedrus and Pausanias are unpassionate and ultimately exterminate *eros*. By subverting it to other things, *eros* does not have its own end in of itself; it is eventually cut off by selfishness (in Phaedrus's account) or morality (Pausanias's account). What is important to realize is that both men also pay homage to Hesiod before beginning their accounts. Phaedrus is explicit and names Hesiod as his authority. Pausanias is slyer but his account of love and mentioning of Aphrodite is lifted from Hesiod's *Theogony* to which he is making indirect references but to which the educated reader will recognize.

The irony of the homages to Hesiod is that the Hesiod of their speeches is nothing more than a figment de-mythologized from his great—if not overly carnal, sensual, and violent—poem. The birth of the gods is through lust, sex, and war. Aphrodite burst forth and rose from the open womb of the sea only after Cronos had castrated Uranus and his phallus had fallen into the sea to give birth to her.

Pausanias's speech, in many ways, builds from Phaedrus. Phaedrus's speech lacked any bonds of relationship to which Pausanias restores or sees as being necessary from Phaedrus's speech. Without morality we cannot survive and thrive, but the love which Pausanias defends is, perhaps to some, also immoral. Phaedrus's pederasty was based on objectified *libido dominandi*. It is rooted in manly domination. Pausanias doesn't disagree, "That is why," he argues, "this Love's inspiration makes people feel affection for what is inherently stronger and more intelligent—which is to say that it makes people incline towards the male" (*Symposium*, 181c).

Unqualified praise, the praise of impetuous desire, is eliminated by the end of Pausanias's speech where praise is not tethered to being controlled. "[T]heir behavior," speaking of the relational bonds of lovers, "—any behaviour—wouldn't warrant criticism, surely, if it were moderate and within the guidelines of convention" (182a). The primacy of νομίμως is how Pausanias ends his discourse on love. Revealing this struggle between nature and convention.

By the end of Phaedrus's and Pausanias's speech, the irony of love's invocation at the beginning is that love has been cut down to size in both accounts. Love has been culled in the service of convention, of law, of regulation. Love has been altogether eliminated from their accounts as selfishness and regulated convention triumph over it.

While Aristophanes was slated to speak next, hiccups cause him to be replaced by Eryximachus. This is intentional on Plato's part because Eryximachus and Aristophanes are dialectical opposites of each other. But in being dialectical opposites, they are also interchangeable as myth gives way to de-mythology and de-mythology is challenged by new mythoi. It is an endless cycle of conflict between mythos and anti-mythos which the *Symposium* itself recapitulates.

Eryximachus represents the hubris of science. He will cite Hesiod like Phaedrus and Pausanias, but his account of the harmony of love in the cosmos is the empty rainbow of modern science. It is a world, paradoxically, devoid of love despite his speech asserting the universality of love pervading the whole cosmos. Moreover, any reader of Hesiod would be baffled by Eryximachus's assertion of the harmony of the gods and the seasonal cycles. Hesiod's world of virility and seasonal cycles is excessively disharmonious. The gods clash with each other in violent ways; Persephone is dragged down to the underworld by Hades to be raped and then released back to earth to signal the arrival of spring only after having been impregnated with (new) life.

Eryximachus's speech is the ultimate culling of love. In his speech, the passionless doctor strips passion from the world while claiming passion pervades all things in a harmonious waltz. Like the Ionian metaphysicians and sophists, Eryximachus has no time for myth, for poetry and the arts, and utterly eviscerates mythoi. He drops the blade of death over Love's head which was the direction set forth by Phaedrus and Pausanias. Love had been placed on trial and found wanting, lacking, and dangerous; the response from Pausanias, Phaedrus, and Eryximachus was to castrate Eros and kick him out into the cold street while claiming to be his disciples or devotees.

This is compounded when Eryximachus assails sacrilege at the close of his speech. His falsity is on display for any educated reader of the poets and the classics. His farce nature, his hubris, now totally revealed. "Sacrilegious behaviour of any kind towards one's parents (alive or dead) and the gods tends to be the consequence of failing to gratify the moderate Love," he says (188c).

The passionate love that is *eros* has been culled to a moderate love; but Eryximachus's condemnation of sacrilege is a condemnation of himself. Eryximachus, more so than Phaedrus and Pausanias, has been the most sacrilegious of speakers.

By the end of Eryximachus's speech Love has been thoroughly de-mythologized by this denizen of science and medicine. For a man supposed to be in the business of protecting life, he has destroyed life. Now the rest of the dialogue is about defending Love, restoring Love, and, in the process, resuscitating life which had been stripped away by the *coup de grâce* of the high priest of the empty rainbow.

Restoring Eros

By the time Aristophanes's hiccups have subsided, the great comic playwright steps up and gives the first memorable and passionate speech in the whole dialogue. Yet he follows the sacrilegious footsteps of Eryximachus. While Phaedrus, Pausanias, and Eryximachus asserted Eros to be the oldest god, Aristophanes does not. But Phaedrus, Pausanias, and Eryximachus killed Eros. Aristophanes may have demoted Eros but is also restoring Eros—or at least trying to resurrect Eros in response to the speeches that came before him.

If Phaedrus, Pausanias, and Eryximachus de-mythologized Eros, then Aristophanes is undeniably re-mythologizing *eros*. Furthermore, Aristophanes is a reactionary. He is reacting against the encroachment of *nomos*, of science and law, of the political, of that regulated morality, against the mad genius and creativity of art and poetry. His passionate speech is also a passionate plea of the importance of art, of poetry, of plays; it is as much a speech made in defense of love as it is in defense of his own profession which is mocked and scorned by philosophers, scientists, and other "enlightened" people who are above the supposed petty and howling superstitions peddled by men like Aristophanes.

Aristophanes's speech is the most carnal, sensual, and sexual of all the speeches. It is the speech of a mad genius. It is the speech of a man of passion who has seen his god put on trial and killed. Now he is lashing out at the world because his beloved idol has been slain.

The literary remarkability of Aristophanes's speech has been well-commented on by scholars and readers for centuries. It is the greatest literary accomplishment of Plato. Although Plato unquestionably makes Aristophanes out to look like a fool, Aristophanes is the first person to get something fundamentally right about love. Love comes from a hole, a wound, a missing link that drives us onward as if exiles looking for a place of serenity and rest.

The mythological speech from Aristophanes may be a myth, but it contains the only truth thus far annunciated in the dialogue. In that sense, what Aristophanes had said is a myth in the truest and most ancient sense: a proclamation. Aristophanes's proclamation, his myth, unlike those proclamations which came before him, contains the first seed of truth in the dialogue.

The irony is that Phaedrus, Pausanias, and Eryximachus—in their de-mythologization of Eros—were the ones who engaged in "myth" in the modern understanding of the term as something untruthful. Those men did not speak truth in their speeches. Their mythos is anti-mythos. Aristophanes's mythos is the mythos that the lover of wisdom naturally grapples with to penetrate the dark unconscious reality of what Aristophanes proclaimed in his ecstatic and rage-filled performance.

There is, nevertheless, a problem with the hyper erotic account of love given by Aristophanes. It is one of agony, of restlessness, and of destruction. The speech has destruction as its central thesis. Love did not spill out into the world with millions of *erotes* filling the world until Zeus split humans in half for their arrogance of challenging the gods. The punishment for sacrilege was the birth of love. It is critically important for Aristophanes to have spoken after Eryximachus because the hubris of the first three speakers who, in feigning platitudes to the gods, challenged the gods. Aristophanes is now the stand in for Zeus, throwing thunderbolts left and right in his speech and wreaking havoc and chaos in the process against his enemies.

Aristophanes was more than a reactionary. He was an iconoclast. His reaction against the death of Eros was to destroy those forces, those institutions, those structures, which had decapitated Eros in the first place. He is the anguished lover taking vengeance for the death and dethronement of his beloved. It was necessary, therefore, for Agathon to be the antithetical corrective to Aristophanes's destructive fury.

Beneath it all, however, Plato's use of comic equivalence through Aristophanes sets the stage for the rest of the dialogue to unfold. Socrates is far from a de-mythologizer. He is equally engaged in the project of re-mythology. After all, his dialogue—the first dialogue after having been preceded by a set of five monologues or speeches—deals with a priestess, mysticism, and the gods. Like Aristophanes, who is reacting violently against the earlier speeches, Socrates deftly rebuts all the previous speeches too. He alludes to all the previous speakers and, in the course of his re-imagined dialogue with Diotima, refutes their propositions (or refutes parts of their propositions while slyly building on whatever grains of truth they may have brought to light).

In the course of the Socratic cross examination with Agathon (who gave the most rhetorically eloquent, beautiful, of the speeches), Socrates exonerates—at least in part—aspects of Agathon and Aristophanes. Socrates agrees that love includes the good which was half of Agathon's speech. Socrates also agrees that love is lacking, which was the central point of Aristophanes's bombastic tirade. The restlessness of Aristophanes becomes the restless pursuit of wisdom in Socrates's speech about Diotima's Ladder. The eloquence and the goodness of Agathon are reassembled to be the good that love seeks in the climb to wisdom.

Plato, through Socrates, is decidedly on the side of the poets. He is not only engaged in a re- mythology against the de-mythologizers, but he also draws on the two partial truths revealed by the mad Aristophanes and the eloquent Agathon, synthesizing the two together in Socrates's most remarkable dialogue and vision which has reverberated through the millennia.

At the same time, Socrates's cross-examination and dialogue on the ladder of *philosophia* is meant to reveal the limits of poetry in its more primeval, ancient, and reactionary form. Despite the half-truths contained in Aristophanes and Agathon, who offered the two most impassioned speeches, their speeches were grounded in rhetoric instead of reason or persuasion. When one is on trial, as Eros is in the dialogue, the defense needs to be persuasive rather than wholly impassioned.

Hence why Socrates's account of love is a persuasive dialogue between seeker and knower who invites the seeker to participate in reason. Socrates does not resort to the overly dramatic rhetoric of Aristophanes or the eloquent rhetoric of Agathon. Instead, Socrates is engaged in the art of *diálogos*. Truth is found in dialogue. Truth is participatory. Truth is in engagement.

Exonerating Eros

By the time Socrates concludes his dialogue he has offered a defense of the importance of *eros* before Alcibiades storms into the gathering in a drunken stupor. Alcibiades enters, as a political figure—the very embodiment of the *polis* and all the force behind it—to act as judge. He judges Socrates the winner. But Socrates, in talking to Aristophanes and Agathon, judges them to be the winner (223c). In having Socrates impregnated, if you will, by Aristophanes and Agathon, Plato is the winner because he is the child born of comedy, tragedy, and philosophy. Can we have multiple winners? Yes.

Plato did not subvert love in the way that Phaedrus, Pausanias, and Eryximachus did because Eros is not the oldest of the gods. Like Aristophanes, Plato accepts Eros as a lower god and a god more intimately bound up in human nature.

With that said, Plato was forced to direct love to something productive rather than restless and destructive. Aristophanes's love and lover are pre-political. Socrates's love and lover are conducive to the political and aid the political. In one massive swoop, Plato demolishes the political aspects of Phaedrus and Pausanias whose accounts of love eventually lead, ironically, to softness and death despite having preached manliness and strength. What irony, all things considered. The constant and always striving ascent in Socrates ensures that love perpetuates into *activa*, or action, upon attaining knowledge which demands us to act and act rightly.

At the end of *The Republic*, Er is resurrected and given knowledge of true reality by the gods and told to return to earth to inform the world of this new knowledge. Plato was a moralist. An ethicist. He was concerned with the primacy of action, of engagement, in a world that was deeply iconoclastic, barbarous, and savage. Love of wisdom allows for the creation of that space where ethical and loving life is possible. This means that *eros* must remain to any understanding of the self, world, and *politeia*. It also means, however, that the energy of love be directed—though not subverted—to productive ends. Eros was on trial in Plato's time. In the course of the dialogue, Plato attempts to defend and exonerate Eros from the de-mythologizers. We are left to judge if he succeeded.

This essay was originally published by *The Imaginative Conservative* under the same title, "Plato's Symposium: The Drama and Trial of Eros," 21 July 2019.

Chapter 10

Virgil's War and Peace

Arma virumque cano (Of arms and the man I sing). So opens Virgil's *Aeneid*, Rome's grandiose epic of a Trojan exile fated by the gods to sojourn across the Mediterranean, sow the seeds of Rome's rivalry with Carthage, and begin the conquest of the Italian Peninsula and plant the spear that would forge the eternal city. For much of Western history, Virgil's *Aeneid* was *the* epic; in fact, T.S. Eliot called it "our classic." The classics, of course, have fallen on hard times, especially Virgil. Is it an epic of unadulterated propaganda to the Augustan regime? Or is it something subtler, even noble, intoxicating, and alluring? Two millennia later, we are still warring over the meaning of Virgil's *Aeneid*.

It is often said that history is written by the victors. Only people who do not know history assert this. Demosthenes was a loser; he organized the Athenian and Theban alliance against Philip II of Macedon and lost, but his speeches have been preserved by posterity, and he remains the indispensable voice of late fourth century ancient Greece. We can even go as far as to say that Plato was a loser, and he wrote the most enduring corpus of Greek literature we have; Plato was no friend of Athenian democracy, and his teacher, Socrates, was condemned to death (yet we remember Socrates and not the men who sentenced him to death). Plato, moreover, was a failed political advisor, yet we still read him as an authoritative voice in political philosophy.

Virgil was the undisputed poet laureate of Rome. Four hundred years after his death, a young Saint Augustine informed his readers in the *Confessions* that he was, as a young student, educated in the poetry of Virgil and wept for Dido while oblivious to the cries of his own soul as a lusty teenager. While Virgil is the most famous of the Augustan poets, another poet named Horace had served as an officer in the armies of Brutus and Cassius that were defeated at Philippi. Horace, of course, wrote a lot too, even though he was on the losing side. The greatest source of the republic's declination is the greatest loser of them all: Cicero.

We know little of Virgil. But if his poetry is reflective of the yearnings of the losers of the Caesarian Civil War; Rome's poet laureate may have been sympathetic to the republican cause. The pastoral idyll, something that Virgil brought to fruition as Arcadia, is the imaginative idyll sung of by everyone from Cicero to Horace to Livy—that famed historian who was considered a sly propagandist rehabilitating Pompey, another one of the losers of the Civil Wars.

When Virgil sings of battle and Aeneas, we are posed with a dilemma. Virgil's entire life had been defined by war. Only after the Augustan settlement was a century of war wiped away and peace consummated. Is Virgil singing that man is, in essence, a warlike creature as he himself experienced and lived through? Or are war and man juxtaposed against each other? Perhaps Virgil was casting war—"a cruel teacher" according to Thucydides and an ever-present danger—as standing in contradistinction to the heart of man? There are two subjects that Virgil sings of in his opening verse: war and man. Are they inextricably interlinked, overlapped but with different aims, or antagonistic to each other but cruelly fated to do battle in the harsh cosmos called life?

Love, History, and War

If we still remember Virgil, it may be because Dante selected him as his guide through hell and purgatory. Why did Dante, a Florentine poet and failed politician, choose a poet who died one and a half millennia ago (at the time of Dante's life) as his guide? Virgil was, for Dante, the great poet of love. And love is one of the major themes of the *Aeneid*.

Amore, pietas, and *laborem* form the trinity of Virgil's governing troika in his infamous epic. In fact, they are all interlinked. Aeneas's love for his father and countrymen is what earns him the epithet pious—or dutiful. But duty is also something laborious. Aeneas labors, and he labors hard. He struggles, in other words, precisely because he loves. He struggles to save his aging father and family as he flees a burning Troy. He struggles against the anger of Juno, Queen of Heaven, to save his family and countrymen as they sail across the stormy seas of the Mediterranean before their landfall in Carthage. He struggles against the desire of his own heart in his falling in love with Dido, Queen of Carthage, whom he must abandon to reach Lavinian shores. He struggles in Italy to secure the land for his countrymen, son, and bride-to-be (Lavinia). All of Aeneas's labors are governed by a dutiful love throughout the epic. Interestingly, praying—not war—is the activity that Aeneas engages in most during the poem.

Yet war is prevalent throughout the epic. Aeneas is driven out to sea by the conclusion of war: the sack and burning of Troy by the Greeks. The final books detail the Trojan invasion of Italy, defended by the spurned Prince Turnus who dies by Aeneas's sword. In Dido's lair, Aeneas recounts the horrifying burning of Troy and killing of Priam; Dido will later kill herself in despair by thrusting Aeneas's sword through her breast and falling atop a smoldering pyre cursing Aeneas and his descendants—thus giving mythopoetic justification for the Punic Wars.

Virgil's construction of the war imagery of the *Aeneid* draws on real historical memory: the memories of the Romans who have a memory filled with the blood and fire of war. Virgil's description of fires, beheadings, and battles would have had a particular resonance with his Roman audience. They would have known all too well what he was alluding to.

In Dido's halls, the Carthaginian Queen—herself an exile—welcomes Aeneas and the Trojans, and the Trojan prince tells her of the final hours of Troy. Here is the first subtle nod to Virgil's beliefs. He associates the recently vanquished Pompey with the memory of the tragic King of Troy.

When Aeneas speaks of "the monarch who once had ruled in all his glory the many lands of Asia, Asia's many tribes. A powerful trunk lying on the shore. The head wrenched from the shoulders. A corpse without a name," he is not only referring explicitly to Priam in this context. He is also alluding to Pompey, that "monarch who once had ruled in all his glory the many lands of Asia" and who, upon his defeat at the hands of Caesar, fled to Egypt where he was beheaded and became "A powerful trunk lying on the shore. The head wrenched from the shoulders. A corpse without a name." That Pompey is tied to Priam, that tragic king of Troy who was immortalized by the Romans, indicates Virgil's hand in seeking to immortalize Pompey just as much as Livy did in his *History*. The eminent classicist Bernard Knox wrote of this subtlety: "Any Roman who read these lines in the years after Virgil's poem was published or heard them recited would at once remember a real and recent ruler over 'the many lands of Asia,' whose headless corpse lay on the shore. It was the corpse of Gnaeus Pompeius (Pompey), who had been ruler of all the lands of Asia."

But Aeneas's erotic rendezvous with Dido is more than a eulogy for Priam (and the Pompeiian republican cause); Virgil humanizes Rome's mortal enemy. Cato the Elder, whenever he finished speaking in the Senate would close his speeches with the infamous words "delendam esse Carthaginem." Carthage was the mortal enemy of Rome, vanquished and turned to a pillar of salt and ash because of the scourging fire of Roman war. Yet Virgil was at the forefront of humanizing and eulogizing Rome's archnemesis, which would reach its fullest fruition in the humane portrayal of Hannibal in Silius Italicus's *Punica*.

As we know, as the Romans knew all too well, the conflict between Carthage and Rome was a result of two clashing cities seeking dominance over the Western Mediterranean. The First and Second Punic Wars had sapped Rome of much of her strength; only a combination of luck and perseverance led Rome to triumph. But Carthage, reduced as she was, remained. While the Third Punic War laid to ash that great city on the North African coastline, the absence of such a worthy enemy became a cause for Roman decline. Almost six centuries later, this sentiment was still echoed by that conflicted Roman bishop of North Africa Saint Augustine.

Romans were raised to hate Carthage. However, Virgil turns Dido into an entirely tragic and human figure, someone whom we—as the Roman audience did—sympathize with. Dido believes Aeneas is a godsend, a heaven-sent match for her sexual loneliness. The two elope on a hunting party and have sex in a cave during a storm. Dido believes this act seals their marriage bond. However, the gods have other plans. Aeneas must not dally and, instead, return to the ships and proceed on his journey to Italy. So the gods intervene and Aeneas flees Carthage leaving Dido weeping and cursing in a storm of pathological emotions.

Dido's death is one of Virgil's greatest accomplishments in the poem. Not only does he humanize the Punic Other that was so reviled in Rome's history; he also draws upon the Third Punic War and its memory to humanize Dido further. Weeping and cursing Aeneas, Dido thrusts Aeneas's blade into her death-devoted heart and falls on a pyre immolating herself. The fact that Dido uses Aeneas's own blades signifies Rome's culling thrust. That she also falls into a burning pyre and is immolated in the flames evokes the memories of Carthage's burning (as well as Troy's burning), which casts Carthage in that sad and tragic light. A great city, a welcoming people, a beautiful queen, vanquished at the hand of sword and fire.

After fleeing Carthage, Aeneas buries his father in Sicily and offers prayers and funeral games in his memory and the memory of the Trojan dead.

The journey continues. On they sail to Italy and make landfall only to find the place inhabited.

The second half of the *Aeneid* details the relationships forged by Aeneas with the locals of Italy, principally the local warrior-prince Pallas, King Latinus, and his daughter Princess Lavinia—which also brings him into a quarreling relationship with Turnus, the leader of the Rutuli peoples who feels spurned having been betrothed to Lavinia.

Turnus is the "Achilles of the West"; he has Greek blood coursing through his veins. Turnus also leads the Latins in their resistance to the Trojans turned Romans. This represents the complicated legacy of Greek colonization in the Italian Peninsula. Prior to Rome, the Italian peninsula was split between the tyrannical Etruscans to the north and the pathological but civilized Greeks in the south (and in Sicily). It is fitting that the great conflict between Aeneas and his Trojans-turned-Romans is against Turnus and his Greek spirit. It is, ironically and paradoxically, the ultimate showdown between the West and East (notwithstanding the fact that the Trojans were easterners who, according to the story, sailed west and then subsequently conquered the East).

The values of *pietas, laborem,* and *amore* are pitted against erotic *thanatos*, the very pathological emotion that leads Turnus to war. When the champions ready their forces for battle, a great melee ensues. Men and women are hacked to pieces. Blood drenches the soil. War has come to Italy.

When Aeneas enters battle, he carries with him into battle—in a nod to Homer—a great shield. Where the shield of Achilles was donned with the imagery of myth, Aeneas's shield is covered in the imagery of history. As we have already been discussing, Virgil relies on historical imagery as his leitmotif to elicit emotion and signification from his Roman audience. Pompey. The Punic Wars. Now Antony and Cleopatra. For the central image on the shield of Aeneas are the bronze ships that fought at Actium and brought to an end the reign of eastern *thanatos* and the triumph of civilized order once more under the banner of Augustus Caesar:

"There is the story of Italy,
Rome in all her triumphs. There the fire-god forged them,
well aware of the seers and schooled in times to come…
the mother wolf stretched out in the green grotto of Mars,
twin boys at her dugs, who hung there, frisky, suckling
without a fear as she with her lithe neck bent back,
stroking each in turn, licked her wolf pups

into shape with a mother's tongue.
Not far from there
he had forged Rome as well and the Sabine women
brutally dragged from the crowded bowl...
And here in the heart
of the shield: the bronze ships, the Battle of Actium,
you could see it all, the world drawn up for war,
Leucata Headland seething, the breakers molten gold.
On one flank, Caesar Augustus leading Italy into battle,
the Senate and people too, the gods of hearth and home
and the great gods themselves...
And opposing them comes Antony leading on
the riches of the Orient, troops of every stripe—
victory over the nations of the Dawn and blood-red shores
and in his retinue, Egypt, all the might of the East
and Bactra, the end of the earth, and trailing
in his wake, that outrage, that Egyptian wife!"

The shield worn by Aeneas, in contrast to the regalia of Turnus, also tells us something important. Aeneas's shield was forged with hard labor, *laborem*, while Turnus is adorned in stolen paraphernalia stripped from those whom he has killed. When Aeneas gets the upper hand against the Achilles of the West, Aeneas is about to take pity on Turnus until he looks down and sees the military belt of his slain friend Pallas. In a moment of rage, Aeneas thrusts the culling blow. Turnus dies, and his soul is dragged off to the underworld. That is where the epic ends, though we know Virgil had not yet finished the epic and even requested it burned right before he died. Luckily, his friends disregarded the last wish of Rome's grandest poet.

What is the impetus of the story at the heart of the *Aeneid*? It is the battle between love and war, between civilization and eros, *laborem* and *thanatos*. Rome wins not because it is more savage than her competitors—though this is historically debatable, that is not the point of poetry—but because the Roman heart is moved with love and, yes, even sympathy. For that is the message being communicated by Virgil's subtle hand.

Aeneas is a man of love. He loves his father. He loves his countrymen. He loves his gods. He is driven across stormy seas and dark caves by the spirit of love manifested in piety, duty. It is his duty as an instrument of the gods—to be sure—but also as a creature of love to bring a civilization rooted in love, *amore*, into existence as the buttress against the death drive of pure erotic *thanatos* that Virgil associates with the Greek East (however fair that is). Pure passion is deadly, as we find out with Dido and Turnus.

However, Virgil does not dehumanize the enemy. On the contrary, Dido and Turnus are sympathetic characters. This, again, is one of the great achievements of Virgil's hand. He turns the hated enemies of Rome into human and sympathetic creatures, humans with a heart and soul that we learn to weep with and for—as Augustine said—while never balking at our relational preference for Aeneas and his desperate band of voyagers and exiles. Turnus, after all, is even described in glowing terms: "his build magnificent." But it is as if Virgil is also singing to his audience that the true spirit of love includes the quality of sympathy. Do not hate, for those who hate curse and bring forth death. Dido and Turnus are the two characters who utter curses of death and, therefore, die. This is true even if we no longer see them from the lens of pure hatred as the Romans of the past had viewed Carthage and Greece.

Dreaming of Peace and Mercy

On the surface, it would seem as if the *Aeneid* is an epic of war. It is, in fact, an epic desiring peace. War and fire surround the epic, but, as the classical tradition is known to us, the underworld revelation is the most significant part of any epic poem.

When in the kingdom of the dead, visiting the heroes of legend and being told the history of the future—which includes the Julii and Augustus Caesar—another image lurks surrounded by the death and historical glory Aeneas sees: the very image that the republican idyll dreamt of, a secluded and peaceful valley with dancing humans governed by peace and joy. Near the end of Aeneas's descent to receive the revelation of what he is laboring for, it is not an image of Roman grandeur but the gentle slopes of a green valley that reveal to us what it is that Virgil is hoping for—and what Aeneas is struggling to achieve:

> *Intersea videt Aeneas in valle reducta seclusum nemus et virgulta sonantia silvae Lethaeumque, domos placidas qui praenatat, amnem. hunc cicum innumerae gentes populique volabant; ac velut in pratis ubi apes aestate serena floribus insidunt variis et candida circum lilia funduntur, strepit omnis murmure campus.*

Meanwhile, in a quiet valley, Aeneas sees a secluded grove and roaring forest thickets and the river of Lethe rippling past many peaceful homes. In the valley danced innumerable peoples and tribes. Out in the meadows, with the blue skies of summer shining overhead, bees land and feast on many-hued blossoms and stream round lustrous flowers and lilies, and all the green pastures murmur with the buzzing and humming of life. [My translation.]

Dancing and joyful humans, singing with the harmonies of nature around them—a multitude of all peoples—is the image of peace that Virgil is singing about. Arcadia, in other words, is the real fruit of Aeneas's labors. It is not the humbling of the proud in war or the formation of civil law and dominion across the Mediterranean. This image, in fact, is the image that truly startles Aeneas, "Struck by the sudden sight, Aeneas, all unknowing, wonders aloud, and asks: 'What is the river over there? And who are they who crowd the banks in such a growing throng?'"

There is plenty of death that surrounds Aeneas in his underworld descent. This image, however, is the exact opposite of the death-devoted heart of Dido, the departed soul of his father Anchises, or the myriad of other dead Romans of history. This startling image is the Arcadian idyll that Virgil believes is the true goal of Roman civilization and the restful and happy place that the human heart—of all tribes and peoples—desires.

This image of a green valley, murmuring and buzzing with life, joyful laughing, and dancing, is the true spirit that guides Virgil. The praise of Augustus Caesar is incidental. Augustus is praised only because he is a mere bridge to the Arcadian idyll and the peace of humans and nature united in a waltz of happiness. Augustus is not praised in the poem at all on this account. He just gets his two cheers for the eternal applause we lavish on this valley of rolling hills and life in its serene joy and harmony which so move the heart and startle us—as it did Aeneas—to know more.

We know that Virgil did not complete the *Aeneid*. *The Aeneid*, as we have it, is an incomplete poem. It is my sincere belief that had Virgil finished the poem we would have witnessed Aeneas, Lavinia, and Ascanius in green valleys, surrounded by tall trees, blossoming flowers, and the humming buzz of bees drinking sweet nectar from the flowers. Peace was the ultimate desire for Virgil and Aeneas. And the ultimate manifestation of that peace—through the blood, fire, and mud of war to be sure—is the Arcadian image that Virgil wrote about in his other poems and gave a revelatory glimpse to Aeneas and all of us in "our classic."

Through blood and war, struggle and pain, death and perseverance, that sacred grove of green pastures and dancing animals is the home we all seek. Arcadia was, after all, the Roman equivalent of what we call Paradise—*parádeisos*, a garden teeming with life. That was the reality that Aeneas's labors aimed for, and it was the reality that Virgil's magnificent epic sought to communicate in alliance with the other republicans who ended up on the losing side of the civil wars. This sliver of paradise is the one place where Aeneas, Dido, and Turnus may finally live the life of loving tranquility denied to them by the decree of fate, history, and the gods.

This essay was first published by *Merion West*, 26 April 2021.

Chapter 11

Finding Arcadia: The Garden in the Cosmos in Latin Literature

Virgil is one of the most common names in Western literature. Apart from the Bible, his writings were perhaps the most read in the history of the West. One cannot read any of the classical creative works of literature, or even works of literary criticism, up through the mid-twentieth century and not find references to Virgil or his voice echoing through the pages.

Virgil's relationship to the political has oscillated between subversive critic of the Augustan regime to sycophantic admirer whose magisterial *Aeneid* was considered the culmination of "the pagan project." While the *Aeneid* is a fixture in the canon of Western civilization, another of Virgil's works has all but been forgotten: the *Eclogues*. Yet Virgil's *Eclogues* rival the *Aeneid*. If the *Aeneid* was the culmination of the pagan political project and the triumph of civilization through naked violence, then the *Eclogues* was the culmination of the pagan desire for serenity in a world often plagued by chaos and violence.

This leads us to the question that has concerned scholars for the last century. Was Virgil a subversive critic of Augustus and the Roman Empire, a sort of proto-romantic reactionary yearning for the republican idyll? Or was he an outright propagandist for Augustus and the new regime that stamped order out of the chaos of nearly a century of war and fratricidal conflict?

I think Virgil was both. Like the other great Latin poets, Horace especially, the praise sung to Augustus was not to Augustus *per se*—as the advocates of the subversive Virgil regularly highlight—but for the Arcadian ideal Augustus allowed to flourish by ending the destructive chaos of war during his rule. The Arcadian idyll is perhaps one of the defining romantic images of Republican Rome. We know the story of Cincinnatus working his little plot of land only to be called back to service to save Rome in her hour of crisis and his return that little sliver of serenity after once again performing his dutiful service for his country. Even Ridley Scott's *Gladiator* portrays the Arcadian idyll when Russell Crowe's General Maximus dies and is reunited with his family in that naturalistic heaven at the close of the film with the tranquility of "Now we are Free" providing a greater *élan vital* to the idyll aesthetic and experience.

It is perhaps inaccurate to call Virgil a Neoplatonist. Virgil's own life would have coincided with what is called Middle Platonism whose greatest representative, Plutarch, was born well after Virgil's death. But what Virgil had in common with the future Neoplatonist was a desire to dwell in the divine realm of nature. The Neoplatonist heart, contrary to popular misconception, did not seek "world flight" but a world-dwelling in the deep roots of the transcendent soul implanted in Nature. The largely ignored *Eclogues* clearly reveal this impulsive desire in Virgil's thought.

Discovering Arcadia

The greatest achievement of the Augustan writers was the creation of traditionalism. It is often said that history is written by the victors. Only someone ignorant of Latin literature could have conjured up such a belief. The greatest Latin writer of all-time, Cicero, was one of the losers of the civil war. Lucan, another great Latin poet, was undeniably sympathetic to the anti-imperial and pro-republican cause. So too, I would contend, were Virgil, Horace, and Silius Italicus. Actual losers, and those sympathetic to the losers, wrote the great histories and poems that have survived from Rome's apogee down to modernity and still inspire generations moved by their aesthetic prose, yearning for peace, and unadulterated celebration of the hedonistic life afforded in Arcadia.

Virgil began composing the poems that comprise the *Eclogues* during the turbulence of the collapse of the Roman Republic and the Caesarian Civil Wars. The poems often oscillate between a pastoral and erotic desire for an idyll with the looming clouds of chaotic urban civilization, "Rome," off in the background. As Meliboeus and Tityrus converse in Tityrus's pastoral home, Meliboeus asks Tityrus who this god is he speaks of as procuring the peaceable pastoral idyll they he enjoys. Tityrus bluntly answers Rome: "*Urbem, quam dicunt Romam, Meliboee [The city, Meliboeus, that they call Rome].*"

It is perhaps paradoxical to think that the great conflagration that was the decline and fall of the Roman Republic also produced the vitality and creativity of Virgil, Horace, Ovid, Cicero, and other luminaries of Latin literature. Yet it is also not hard to understand why. In the turbulence and turmoil, the educated elite in Roman society yearned for a restoration and a return to their agrarian idylls which had been shattered by mass marches, revolts, and decades of war. Only as their world was fading away did they come to realize with such passionate intensity how much they loved it.

After all, Tityrus and Meliboeus enjoy pleasant friendship and peaceable conversation in the first *Eclogue*—something far removed from tales of flight, fight, and storms.

> "Happy old man!" Meliboeus interjects, "Here, amid familiar streams and sacred springs, you shall enjoy the cooling shade. On this side, as of old, on your neighbor's border, the hedge whose willow blossoms are sipped by Hybla's bees shall often with its gentle hum soothe you to slumber; on that, under the towering rock, the woodman's song shall fill the air; while still the cooing wood pigeons, your pets, and the turtle dove shall cease not their moaning from the elm tops."

The image is quintessentially serene.

The ultimate end of this pastoral idyll is a humanization of the wedding banquet of Peleus and Thetis—minus all the strife. "Yet this night," Tityrus says, "you might have rested here with me on the green leafage. We have ripe apples, mealy chestnuts, and a wealth of pressed cheeses." Rome has won this peace and bountiful harvest for men to enjoy. For that reason, Rome is a god. But the god that is Rome is also kept at distance. Tityrus doesn't pray to this god. He prays to the muses, stags, and starlight that he intimately dwells with. That is what governs and guides his heart. He acknowledges what provides this idyllic serenity, but he doesn't worship it as he does the Arcadian paradise he calls home.

Ironic Praise

Virgil, like his Greek forebears, was also something of an ironist. Aeneas is driven away from his ancestral homes and into the tumult of the sea by capricious gods who also deny his desire to wed Dido and leave a comfortable and pleasurable life on the shores of Carthage. Aeneas, traveling to the underworld, hears the prophecies of the coming of Rome and the son of Jupiter, Augustus, ruling over the world.

The Aeneid is a poem of strife and war. It is also a poem celebrating the new ideology in the Augustan Empire: *pietas*. *Pietas*, in Latin, means duty.

English derives the word piety from it. But while we envision gentle grandmothers praying rosaries, the Roman understanding of *pietas* was imbued with a spirit of masculine struggle and duty: duty to honor the gods, protect your family, and serve your fellow countrymen.

But such a life of constant struggle, as Tityrus implies, is not worth living. We want the idyll. We seek the serenity offered within it. We desire the sumptuous. None of this is possible through the constant laborious struggles of *pietas*. Augustus will bring peace, yes—this is undoubtedly a good thing— but what is better than Augustus's mere *Pax Romana* is the Arcadian idyll of beauty, joy, and peace; the luscious "canopy of a spreading beech, wooing the woodland Muse on slender reed" is what Virgil really sings praise of. As such, Augustus is a mere instrument, a means, to an even greater end. Augustus, ironically, gets passed by as we approach the Arcadian Paradise that calls Virgil home.

When Aeneas travels into the underworld in the sixth book of the *Aeneid*, the usual descent beyond the realm of the living to experience the transcendent mysteries of esoteric knowledge, it is not so much the prophecy of Augustus that this descent reveals to us but the vision of the Elysian fields—Arcadia— that is true culmination of this revelatory sojourn:

> *Intersea videt Aeneas in valle reducta seclusum nemus et virgulta sonantia silvae Lethaeumque, domos placidas qui praenatat, amnem. hunc cicum innumerae gentes populique volabant; ac velut in pratis ubi apes aestate serena floribus insidunt variis et candida circum lilia funduntur, strepit omnis murmure campus.*

> [Meanwhile, in a quiet valley, Aeneas sees a secluded grove and roaring forest thickets and the river of Lethe rippling past many peaceful homes. In the valley danced innumerable peoples and tribes. Out in the meadows, with the blue skies of summer shining overhead, bees land and feast on many-hued blossoms and stream round lustrous flowers and lilies, and all the green pastures murmur with the buzzing and humming of life.] [My translation]

Dancing humans joyfully singing, green forests and rushing waters, and humming and buzzing bees are all seamlessly interwoven together in an unforgettable image of beauty and harmony. This image—this image of joyous peace with man and nature as one—is the true revelation for Aeneas, not the prophecy of Augustus. This image, this image of Arcadia, is what Aeneas is destined to bring for his descendants. Arcadia—these Elysian fields—is what Aeneas is fighting and struggling for.

This image provided by Virgil in the *Aeneid* also helps us understand some of the praise and proto-romantic poetry of Horace. Horace was a hedonist. In his biography of Horace, Suetonius writes, "[Horace] is said to have been exceptionally intemperate in his love affairs, and there is a story that he so disposed his lovers in a mirrored room that whichever way he looked, there was a reflection of sexual intercourse." It is unsurprising that Horace's poetry often blurs the lines between sex, love, and lust—but reading Horace also reveals his distaste for fratricidal civil wars and urban progress which destroys the very agrarian idyll which makes the hedonistic life possible.

The contempt that Horace has for civil war—being a man, living from 65 B.C. to 8 B.C., who lived through the constant tumult for much of his life under the aftermath of the Battle of Actium—is readily visible in his poetry:

> "Surely if any man shall wish to put an end
> to impious slaughter and the madness of civil strife,
> if he shall wish his statues
> to be inscribed 'Father of Cities,' let him have courage
> to rein back our wild license."

The horror of war constantly grieves Horace: "Back to war, Venus, after all / these years? Spare me, spare me, I beg you." War has ruined Horace's life, destroyed the idyll, and has made the pleasurable life impossible:

> "As for me, I no longer take pleasure in a woman
> or boy, nor in the fond hope that my love might still
> be returned, nor in drinking bouts,
> not in binding my brow with fresh flowers."

Horace goes further in describing war as "mad." The madness of war is incomprehensible to him. Men like Julius Caesar, Pompey the Great, and Crassus, who thrived on war and sought war to win the praises and acceptance of the republican establishment, utterly horrified him. The madness of war is naturally contrasted with the romanticized Arcadian idyll that was reemerging under Augustus but still threatened by the urbanization of Rome and the broader Italian peninsula:

> "But when the thunder of Jove's winter season
> musters the rains and snows, with all his dogs on every side he drives
> wild boar into his ring of nets,
> or stretches wide-meshed toils on twigs he's smoothed
> to trap the greedy thrushes,

and hunts the timid hare and crane migrating
to his snare—delicious prey.
Amid these pleasures who would not forget
the miseries brought on by love?"

When Horace praises Augustus, like Virgil, the emperor is merely an
instrument to be passed by—a shield of peace, to be sure, but not the real focus
of the poet's adoration:

"I was eager to sing of battles and defeated cities,
But Phoebus struck his lyre and forbade me
To sail my little boat
Across the Tyrrhenian sea. Your Augustan age,
Caesar, has given rich crops back
To our fields, has brought the standards back to our Jupiter,
Tearing them from the proud door posts
Of the Parthians...
While Caesar is guardian of the state, neither civil war
Nor civil madness will drive away our peace,
Nor will anger beat out its swords
And set city against unhappy city."

The end of war is a good. And insofar that Augustus brought about the
"civil madness" that drives peace away, Horace has good things to say (let us
never forget Horace fought against Augustus at Philippi). But Augustus is
never the true subject of Horace's praise poetry. Arcadia is.

Pilgrimaging to Arcadia

This desire for the Arcadian idyll is inherited even by Christianity. Saint
Augustine of Hippo was, at one level, the harshest critic of the emptiness of
the Roman ideology in the ancient world. In the *City of God*, Augustine
exhaustively critiqued the propagandistic ideology of Roman exceptionalism
—laying to bare for all to see. Despite Augustine's critical indictment against
Rome's lust to dominate the world and bringing untold misery to millions in
its wake, Augustine stops short of condemning political order altogether.

In Book 19 of the *City of God*, Augustine gives what stood as the most
consequential political theology in Christian history—at least until the Second
Vatican Council. There is a temporal good that is universal to pagan and
Christian alike which politics provides. It is altogether not dissimilar from the
praise of peace found in Virgil and Horace. Peace, Augustine argues, is the
great good that benefits all and that all aim for: "Anyone who joins me in an

examination, however slight, of human affairs, and the human nature we all share, recognizes that just as there is no man who does not wish for joy, so there is no man who does not wish for peace."

From this perspective, the Second Vatican Council goes deeper into Augustine's vision of the mission of the Church in the world for the great bishop wrote,

> "Thus even the Heavenly City in her pilgrimage here on earth makes use of the earthly peace and defends and seeks the compromise between human wills in respect of the provisions relevant to the mortal nature of man, so far as may be permitted without detriment to true religion and piety. In fact, that City relates to the earthly peace to the heavenly peace, which is so truly peaceful that is should be regarded as the only peace deserving the name, at least in respect of the rational creation; for this peace is the perfectly ordered and completely harmonious fellowship in the enjoyment of God, and of each other in God."

The Church as peacemaker—"blessed be the peacemakers"—is also for an even greater end: the true Arcadian idyll that is the beatific peace in God.

As the Vandals were sweeping through North Africa, Augustine upbraided Count Boniface—the Roman general and master of the soldiers in Africa—for his dereliction of duty. Augustine and Boniface were friends. Boniface, in fact, had sought to retire from the army and join a monastery but Augustine talked him out of it so that he may provide the peace that so many of his fellow citizens benefited from. As Boniface dithered and refused to face the Vandals, Augustine excoriated him for lack of Christian charity in upholding his vows to Rome to provide peace and security in North Africa, "Do not think that it is impossible for anyone to please God while engaged in active military service."

Augustine, the great critic of Rome and the emptiness of politics in the first half of the *City of God*, is not contradicting himself in the latter half of the *City of God* or in his letters to Boniface. Augustine does not see—as Virgil and Horace did—the temporal peace wrought by the force of Rome as providing the serenity that all humans desired. Augustine goes even further than that.

Imperfect as Rome was, and it most certainly was in Augustine's critique, it nevertheless provided a sense and space and temporal order for the journey to Arcadia, the true Arcadia, the New Eden where the "only peace deserving the name" existed and the true joy that all humans seek is actualized. Augustine's praise of the peace won in temporal politics, as in Virgil and

Horace, is a praise that aims beyond the political. The reason why peace is good is because it allows us to sojourn to Arcadia, to find that true peace and joy all humans seek. This is what political order ought to allow for us. In more modern parlance, from a man who was steeped in the classical tradition, "life, liberty, and the pursuit of happiness." But that life, liberty, and pursuit of happiness would eventually lead to the discovery of a garden.

Horace shares with Augustine this instinctive desire for Arcadia—the land of bountiful joy, peace, and serenity:

> So let us seek the Blessed Fields and Wealthy Isles,
> where every year the land unploughed gives grain,
> and vines unpruned are never out of flower,
> and olive shoots unfailing bud, and set their fruit,
> and dusky fig ungrafted graces its own tree,
> the honey flows from hollow ilex, and from hills
> the streamlet lightly leaps with sounding footfall.
> There to the milking pails unbidden come the goats,
> and friendly flocks their swollen udders bring.
> When evening comes no howling bear patrols the pens,
> no viper heaves its mound of earth.
> Enchanted, we shall wonder at it all."

It is now unmistakable that what really governs the heart of Latin literature, from the pagan poets to the Christian artists whom we call theologians: the green pastures with all their ripening fruit and flowers bestowing peace and happiness to mankind. In that garden, as Augustine says, "How great shall be that felicity, which shall be tainted with no evil, which shall lack no good, and which shall afford leisure for the praises of God, who shall be all in all!" In that garden, the New Eden, the chaos of the cosmos finds its calm. It that garden, the restless heart of man finds it final and perfect rest.

Ad Astra

What the politics of Latin literature confers to us is the desire for peace and joy, a peace and joy found in an intimate environment of beauty which the poets, even theologians, described as a garden. They do not praise the generals or emperors or consuls as such. When they are praised these offices are merely a passing instrument, the people who attained peace and allowed the Arcadian idyll to become a reality, however fleeting.

The Golden Age of Latin Literature and running through its nadir with the collapse of Rome, finds itself replete with the same symbolism from the pagans to the Christians. Our world is often beset by chaos and strife, disorder and civil unrest, but in the midst of it there is the yearning and journeying to a peace and serenity that calls us all and brings healing and wholeness to friendships, cities, and sinful human beings. The taste of that reality, which is always found in peace, sets us on the journey for that new horizon.

But the greater wisdom, however terrifying, is that the race to Arcadia runs through strife, war, and murder. That fact makes the Arcadian idyll even more desirable. So, like Dante, we find ourselves on that same hallowed path our forebears tread:

> "From those holiest waters I returned
> to her reborn, a tree renewed, in bloom
> with newborn foliage, immaculate,
> eager to rise, now ready for the stars."

In that journey we might just find, as Dante did, the echoes of Virgil by our side as we realize the love that guides the cosmos is intimately bound up with the reality of a garden with the luminescent stars of Latin writers—pagan and Christian alike—illuminating that garden as we journey to it.

This essay was first published by *Front Porch Republic* on 10 June 2021.

Chapter 12

Fallen From Eden:
Reading the Poetry of Catullus

Catullus is the most difficult of the Roman poets to wrestle with. For one, he is mostly a mystery compared to his contemporaries and successors like Horace, Virgil, and Ovid. Moreover, what poetry of his survives sometimes comes across as obscene in a way that not even the writings of Ovid or Horace do. Recent scholars like C.J. Fordyce consider a third of his 117 poems unworthy for reflection: their obscenity speaks for itself. Yet Catullus is the creator of Latin elegiac poetry, his lyricism is unarguably breathtaking and witty (in the Latin), and he was an individual who sang of what Christians identified as man's fallen nature: that tension between love and lust, compassion and hatred, joy and envy. Catullus, then, may be the preeminent poet of the city of man, but his poems also move with the spirit of a restless soul seeking the nourishment that only Love itself can provide.

"I hate and I love, why do I so, perhaps you ask? / I do not know, but I feel it, and I am crucified" (Poem 85). This short poem encapsulates the totality of Catullus's poetry. Love and hate, confusion and torment, desire and guilt. In two lines Catullus poetically summarized the human condition's many twists and turns.

Catullus lived through turbulent and transformative times. He lived and died during the nadir of the Roman Republic. He counted such luminaries as Cicero, Crassus, Pompey, and Julius Caesar as his contemporaries. He made fun of them all, at least to the degree that he could without losing his life (and occasionally having to apologize to stay in their good graces). He was, in this regard, somewhat courageous in taking on the Roman power players during the republic's terminal decline into civil war and empire (which he did not live to see). In this chaotic time, as we also know, he fell madly in love with "Lesbia," Clodia Metelli, wife of the Roman politician and consul Quintus Caecilius Metellus Celer. His love for Clodia, and his witnessing the real time decline of the Roman Republic, fueled his most memorable poetry: his love poetry to Clodia and his reflection on the decline of the ages (his famous "Bedspread poem," Poem 64). It is, therefore, these poems that I wish to concentrate on and through them offer a penetrating critique and appraisal of Catullus's heart—a heart that we too share even if we think ourselves primmer and more proper than Catallus's own fantastical imagination and tumultuous life.

When Catullus wrote those words: "I hate and I love," he spoke true words about the human condition. While one can say that it was also a manifestation of Catullus's own life—specifically his failed love life which saw Clodia fade away from his bedside clutch and that no other woman held such a place as she in his heart—the agonized love and lust which Catullus speaks of in his poetry is something that philosophers, theologians, and writers of the past and present have wrestled with. We all intuitively know that this agonized love, this trepidatious line between joy and enmity, is something deeply real as we have all experienced it in our lives. Catullus, then, speaks to us in our most hopeful moments. He also speaks to us in our crudest and darkest moments. This is what makes Catullus engaging and repulsive simultaneously.

*

The tension between love and hate is not merely found in his love poems to Clodia. The tension between love and hate is the central theme of Poem 64 as we slide through the myth of the ages toward decline: the impossibility of love and the agonizing heartbreak of having fallen from that primordial grace of blissful existence without suffering the broken heart of a lover sailing away from our lives forever.

Poem 64 opens with the memories of an Edenic-like paradise, Arcadia to the Romans, with its picturesque depiction of nature which also evokes the goddess Minerva: "They say that pines were born long ago / From the head of Mount Pelion in Thessaly / And swam the sea, its undulating waves / To Phasis, pheasant river, and / The land of Aeetes the king." The poem begins with this depiction of serenity and the joy of Peleus and Thetis, father and mother to the great hero Achilles (more on him later).

In the wedding banquet, Catullus ignores the story of Pseudo-Apollodorus where the goddess of discord (Eris) was excluded and tossed the apple of discord into the banquet which caused the goddesses Minerva

(Athena), Juno (Hera), and Venus (Aphrodite) to war with each other and demand a verdict as to who was the most beautiful. Instead, Catullus depicts the wedding that everyone yearns for: pure love, joy, and the bliss that comes with wedding garments and song. It is the ideal within the idyll.

However, the wedding of Peleus and Thetis that gives birth to the heroes "most admired / Beyond measure of all Ages," quickly descends from that golden age into decay. "The place [that] was filled / With the jubilant crowd who held gifts before their faces / And faces expressing joy," is contrasted with the imagery of uncleansed soil and fallen leaves polluting the fields causing "decay" to "over[u]n the abandoned ploughshares." The hour of happiness is also the hour of decline. The poem shifts to the story of heroes: Theseus and Ariadne and Achilles.

The myth of the ages asserted that the decline from gold to silver to bronze was given a brief respite in the heroic age. The heroic age brought new life, new inspiration, new vitality to the world of decadence and destruction. Here Catullus brilliantly subverts this portrait and continues with his own "fall of man" in the continual decline of the earth and humanity.

Catallus's continued progression of the bedspread poem inverts our expectations as well as implying the tragedy of love and the sorrow that comes with a love unfulfilled. Peleus and Thetis should now enter the bed to consummate their love with each other in the rapturous bliss that comes with marriage. This was the hope of Ariadne (who can be understood to be Catullus in real life) with Theseus (sometimes considered to be Clodia in real life). Ariadne's dreams of marriage to Theseus are shattered when the hero abandons her and sails away to Crete to meet King Minos and eventually set sail for Attica where he will slay the infamous Minotaur that enslaves the people there and become the mythical hero-king founder of Athens.

But the concentration on Theseus forgets Ariadne. Catullus includes, in brief, Theseus's feats, but he concentrates on the lament and sorrow of Ariadne, spurned and abandoned by Theseus, her heart fading into oblivion, her tears cascading down her cheeks like a torrential waterfall, beaten and broken by the false promises of love which causes enmity between the sexes. The loss of love causes her to be "pitiful and alone on lonely sands" which shatters her "hope for…a happy marriage" dancing under the stars with those "Longed-for wedding songs."

Here Catullus, knowingly or not, speaks truth about love and the lack thereof. Love binds together, as we saw with Peleus and Thetis. Love initially bound Ariadne and Theseus together. If love binds together, if love is the "unitive force" that holds all things together, the opposite of love is separation. Separation leads to loneliness. The loss of love for Ariadne results in precisely that: separation from Theseus which results in her utter isolation: she is alone "on lonely sands." As Ariadne watches Theseus sail away, her heart still desires to cling to him—a reflection of her still unquenched though dying love for the hero—but is now "completely lost" reminding us of that isolation and loneliness that comes with a love unconsummated.

The "raging" "passion in her heart" leads to her lament. Ariadne's lament is a heartfelt plea, a curse, really, directed against Theseus with significant implications. She curses him and his false promises which extends into a more universal statement of enmity between the sexes: "May no woman now believe a man where he makes a promise / May no woman hope the words of her man are true." We grieve for Ariadne because we, too, know the loss of love and the heartbreak that comes with it. Ariadne's sorrow and lament reveal her love, but it also reveals the "hate" that comes with a love spurned and rejected.

The other great hero that Catullus subtly inverts, and critiques, is Achilles—the child of the love between Peleus and Thetis which the poem began with. Catullus's critique of Achilles is the perfect continuation of the imagistic language he has crafted with the abandonment of Ariadne. The loss of love that Ariadne experiences is now met with the imagery of bloodshed and destruction as Catullus launches into the infamous rage of Achilles where he storms back into battle and causes the Scamander River to flow red with blood: "For as a reaper picks thick bundles of corn / Beneath the blazing sun and harvests the blond fields, / So [Achilles] will lay low the bodies of the Troy-born / With unforgiving iron … The River Scamander will witness his great virtues / As it flows in profusion … [with] Slaughtered bodies that mount up."

Catullus is satirical about the "great virtues" of Achilles. What great virtue lies in death and destruction? None at all. Having witnessed the sorrow of Ariadne's abandonment and lament, this sorrow of a love lost turns into the imagery of death and destruction with the pivot to Achilles. Catullus is magnificent in the dialectical progression of how the loss of love leads to death, and he does so with a piercing satirical critique of the greatest hero of antiquity. Achilles is no hero. Just as Theseus is no hero. (At least from Catullus's critique within the poem.)

The arc of the bedspread poem is the gradual decline from the golden age of Arcadian bliss and serenity to the sorrow of love spurned to the death and destruction that results because of the impossibility to find happiness and solace in love. This is the age we now find ourselves in according to Catullus (notwithstanding the fact that Catullus himself was unable to consummate the burning love of his own heart). Moreover, where the heroic age was generally conceived and imagined as a time of reprieve and inspiration, Catullus subtly implies that it was yet another continuation in the declination of humanity. So now the "gods [have turned] away from us. / So they do not dignify our assemblies with their presence, / Or even bear to touch the clear light of day."

What begins in a serene and joyful opening—Arcadia with the wedding of Peleus and Thetis—moves to heartbreak, sorrow, death, and destruction. Poem 64 follows the myth of the ages, but Catullus inverts the heroes and heroic age as just another path on the decline; it is a lamentable age, an age of betrayal, deceit, and skullduggery. The heroic age brought grief and death, not respite and new life. Those who worship the heroic age blind themselves to its reality: the sorrow of Ariadne, the bloodthirsty rage of Achilles, and the death that came from love spurned. What a depiction of the fall of man.

*

Beyond the bedspread poem, Catullus is most famously remembered for his love poems to Clodia ("Lesbia") as hitherto mentioned. It is easy to dismiss these poems as the ruminations of a man-child who never grew up, a lovesick puppy angry that the love he sought was not reciprocated, and the often-obscene language seems to warrant its rejection on that ground alone. Such dismissal of Catullus's poetry, however, misses the profound insights that Catullus provides into the turbulence of love and lust and the dream that "love" can "last forever."

Love has the power to unite and bring serenity in a world of flux and violence. It transports us back to that original Edenic, Arcadian, paradise that we have fallen from. Our language today, like Catullus's language then, still evokes this idyll in love. Clodia is the "sparrow" and "apple" of Catullus's eye. Their love is like the "Libyan sand," kissing and caressing each other on the golden beaches with the soft waves of the ocean crashing up around them. The experience of love always seems to take us back to that primordial garden where love was first sanctified under the skies of purity, waves of serenity, and leaves of the trees.

How often, like Catullus, do we see in our culture—literature and film especially—romantic moments under the sun, the moon, and the stars? How often, like Catullus, do we have our own experiences of love in the blessed meadows and fields of nature? How often, like Catullus, do our sacred traditions evoke Eden, gardens of delight, and blossoming flowers as the pasture in which love is most fully realized?

But all that glistens is not gold.

Catullus, being the man he was, was also attune to the madness and ecstasy of love turned to lust. From those same images of sparrows and apples and grains of Libyan sands, Catullus also speaks of loosening "chastity belt[s]" for "a thousand kisses" and "another thousand" that cause him to go "crazy" and become "a fool" and "failure." Here, too, Catullus reaches into the dark id of human existence and its libidinal desires that can lift us into that Arcadian paradise of blissful love or tear us down and drag us into the abyss of "hate," cruelty, and anger:

> Lesbia says a lot of cruel things to me in front of her husband.
> The dolt finds considerable happiness in this.
> Mule, do you have no feelings? If she had forgotten me and kept quiet
> She would be cured. But since she barks and abuses
> Not only does she remember me but – this is far more piercing –
> She is angry. This is how it is, she burns, and she talks.

Like many lovers, Catullus employs an inverse psychological justification of how taunting teasing and cruelty is itself a reflection of love. This is the madness of love—really, lust—which drives us insane and often is the catalyst for abuse. "Lesbia always speaks badly of me," Catullus writes, but in that speaking "badly" of him, the lovesick poet interprets these moments as evidence of her love: "I'll be damned if Lesbia does not love me. / How can I tell? Because with me it's just the same. / I curse her continuously, / But I'll be damned if I do not love her."

Catullus's juxtaposition of the serenity of love with the madness of hate, cruelty, and anger is also something common in our cultural patrimony. How often, like with Catullus, do we see in our culture—literature and film especially—lovers quarrel with one another, strike each other, and engage in cruel teasing and mockery that sometimes results in physical confrontation? How often, like Catullus, do we know people in such relationships where things seem romantically ideal at one moment then horrifying terrible in the next? How often, like with Catullus, do our sacred traditions also depict the tension between love and hate burning up in our own souls and hearts, the temptations and turbulence that comes with the restless heart seeking love while fighting against the death-impulse of lust?

Catullus may not have understood lust in the way that those who came after him did, but we have the benefit of living in the aftermath of those writers and thinkers who were able to separate the bliss of love (which Catullus correctly identifies with the serenity of that primordial perfection) from the destructive anger and danger of lust (which Catullus says he is incapable of knowing though he senses and is tormented by it). As such, we can see in Catullus the twists and turns of the tempestuous soul caught in the rapturous vicissitudes of life crying out for that grace which is love while being drowned in a torrential whirlpool of his own *libido dominandi*. We see in Catullus our own personal struggles and hopes, our vanity and ego, our failures and our want for redemption. Catullus's love poems sing of this common mortal condition we all inhabit. Good and bad.

If love is the calming medicine of the soul that brings unity and serenity in the midst of death and destruction, a union of two become one, Catullus still glimpses that reality:

You dangle before me, my love, and life, the prospect
That this love of ours will be cherished and last forever.
Great gods, make it that she can promise truthfully,
And say it sincerely and from her heart
So that we may live our whole lives
By this everlasting pact of sanctified love.

*

It would be a great injustice to our own lives if we discard Catullus simply on the grounds of his crudity and paedomorphic antics and language scattered throughout his poems. Yet have we not, ourselves, cried the same feelings of Catullus? Have we not been caught in the ecstatic torment of love and our want to consummate it and the grief and sorrow of love's failure? Have we not ourselves cried out to the heavens for sanctification and for those dreams of living a loving life in a garden of delights to come true? If we run from Catullus, it is only because we see too much of our darker selves in him while remaining blind to those wondrous moments of light that break out of his wicked splendor and lift us back to that original bliss we yearn for.

Catullus is not a saint. He is not a moral poet. But his crudity and madness still dance with the shadows of truth and echo with the cry of the human heart. He is entirely right that we should cry out to the "Great gods" so that those whom we love can "sincerely" declare it "truthfully" "from [their] heart" and out of this declaration of love two lives will come together through that "pact of sanctified love" that will "last forever."

Despite it all, Catullus is right to see love as life: "We should live, my Lesbia, we should love." Only in that love do we experience the calming heart of joy that gives us a taste of eternity. For all his many faults and ills, Catullus still glimpsed that serenity of eternity offered in love where blossoming flowers, golden sand, and cascading waves don't weep in sorrow but sing in happiness.

This essay was first published at *Front Porch Republic*, 10 November 2021.

Chapter 13

Is Ovid Still Worth Reading?

In the annals of Roman poets, Ovid occupies a unique place. He is generally regarded as inferior to Virgil, Rome's grandest and grandiose poet whose *Aeneid* still stands as Rome's mythopoetic masterpiece and whose *Eclogues* set the stage for the development of the pastoral idyll in Western literature. Yet Ovid's language and picturesque scenes strike one as occasionally more remarkable and energetic than Virgil; Edward Gibbon, for instance, said he derived more pleasure reading Ovid than the other Latin poets. Ovid, however, strikes moderns as dangerous and out of date. His poems on sexual violence, often tinging with toxic masculinity, don't necessarily fit the sensibilities of our post-MeToo age. But such readings of Ovid fail to see the grander portrait, even the dark wisdom, found in the *Metamorphoses*.

The Metamorphoses is an epic of transformation, of change. Like Pseudo-Apollodorus's *Bibliotheca*, Ovid's *Metamorphoses* is a collection of the grandstanding myths of Antique culture, especially as inherited in the Latin-Roman tradition. It opens with the birth of the cosmos, its wrestling into order from chaos which provided the basis for life and all the subsequent stories that the poem sings of. It concludes with a summary of the great stories that moved pagan consciousness, finishing with the apotheosis of Julius Caesar, the expansion of the walls of Rome and Roman civilization with it (echoing Virgil), and Ovid's own declaration that his fame will live on for all eternity because of the "truth" "stablished by poetic prophecy" that he himself is the avatar of. We'll return to this point later.

Yet Ovid doesn't celebrate, upon closer inspection, the mighty walls of Rome as do his contemporaries. Ovid pays his due respect to Rome, but Rome must submit to the winds and cosmos of change; time changes all things, Rome is no exception. This is why Ovid leads up to his conclusion by including the speeches of Pythagoras, the great Greek philosopher who argued that in the cosmos of time that changes all things only one thing remains the same in the midst of this torrential sea of change: the soul. Ovid's *Metamorphoses*, then, is an inspection into the soul that never changes; and in that inspection Ovid finds the tension between love and lust, beauty and ugliness, death and redemption, sorrow and happiness. The soul may experience changes wrought by its burdening enslavement to the oceans of time, but what the soul seeks is the same: constancy through love, the eternity which never changes because love never changes.

I shall examine, here, but a few of the many stories included in Ovid's great epic of the human soul. Each embody their own unique particularities. Each also reflect the great spirit of prophetic song that Ovid wanted us to know as the only constancy in our lives full of flux.

*

Cadmus, as we know, was one of the great early Greek heroes before the time of Hercules and the mythical founder of Thebes, the first of the grandest city-states of Greece where it can be said Greek culture was born. The son of King Agenor of Tyre, when Jupiter (Zeus) stole Europa out of lust, Cadmus was sent west to retrieve his sister under the threat of permanent exile. Cadmus complies out of love of his father and love for his sister but fails.

The heart of Cadmus, however, is eventually rewarded for his love and piety. Journeying west in pursuit of Jupiter to find Europa, he eventually comes across the fertile ravines, plains, and hills of Boeotia. He kneels before the oracle of Apollo, an act of loving piety, and upon hearing the oracular prophecy and finding the land he will soon settle and call his new home, he gives thanks again to the gods and makes a sacrifice to Jove.

Companions of his are sent out to retrieve clean water for the ritual. They encounter the dragon, a large snake, and are devoured by the predatory beast. Worried about the whereabouts of his brethren, Cadmus strikes out to find them and discovers the beast: "Its crest sh[ining] gleaming gold; its eyes flash[ing] fire." The monstrous dragon and Cadmus soon do battle with Cadmus emerging victorious. There, Pallas Minerva arrives and commands Cadmus to bring into existence a people and city. Planting the teeth and blood of the slain dragon into the soil, up springs the warriors of Thebes and the protectors of Boeotia born out of the death of the serpent.

The trials and labors of Cadmus conclude with his marriage to Harmonia, daughter of Mars and Venus. Harmonia, of course, means harmony. They have many children together. While the eventual demise of Cadmus and

Harmonia is described later, as Cadmus is turned into a snake as is Harmonia, their transformations into snakes to slither and wander the world not as predatory monsters but as loving companions brings solace to the story. Love binds together, even if in fantastical imagery as Ovid recounts for us. Cadmus and Harmonia come together in love in Boeotia; their love is stronger than mere physical attraction to beauty for even when Cadmus is metamorphosized into a snake, Harmonia will not abandon her husband and is transformed with him. Despite all the transformations that occur around them, the soul of love remains constant between Cadmus and Harmonia even as they themselves are altered.

*

The transformation of Cadmus and Harmonia is followed by the story of Perseus and Andromeda, one of the most famous stories of antiquity. We know it well through cultural inheritance even if we haven't spent the time to read the classical stories of mythology. Paintings throughout the Western world depict the events of Perseus's life, and Perseus is still a hero in film as seen in *The Clash of the Titans* and its recent remakes.

It is cheap and easy to read the story of Perseus and Andromeda as one of male sexual fantasy and the masculine and misogynistic trope of the heroic male securing his bride who is the damsel in distress. Such politicized readings of the last fifty years miss the profundity of Ovid's inclusion of the story in his grander poetic agenda of love being the constant star in the midst of a world of violence and transformation.

Andromeda is chained to a rock, doomed to be eaten by a sea monster because of the haughtiness of her mother. Cassiopeia challenges the divinities, the naiads, that Andromeda is more beautiful than they. Neptune (Poseidon) is enraged by this irreverence (irreverence, a lacking in love, is often a catalyst for darkness and death throughout the *Metamorphoses*). Neptune steals Andromeda and chains her to a rock in the sea to meet her fate.

Meanwhile, the gorgon Medusa was transformed into her serpent-like monster form by offending Minerva (Athena) by seducing Neptune and having sex inside Minerva's temple (as goddess of wisdom and virginity, the act defiles Minerva's temple). Medusa considered herself to be the most beautiful creature in the world. Minerva forcefully takes revenge for this impiety by turning Medusa's beautiful flowing hair into snakes and by turning the gaze of men into a moment of death: whereas before men could have looked upon Medusa's face and been enraptured by her beauty, now men who look upon Medusa's face die as they turn to stone.

So enters Perseus in the midst of a drama caught up by irreverence as a dithering fiancé (Phineus) whose only interest in Andromeda was to secure advancement in royal lineage and power. What, then, makes Perseus stand out compared to all the other actors in this story? Where Cassiopeia and Medusa are irreverent and punished because of it, Perseus is pious and reverent by contrast. Before Minerva he trusts (*fides*, has faith) the goddess and her revelation of how to defeat Medusa. Where Cassiopeia and Medusa are vain, Perseus is humble; where sexual lust leads to danger and destruction, Perseus is more interested in getting to know the soul of Andromeda despite her obvious carnal beauty: "When Perseus saw her, had a wafting breeze / Not stirred her hair, her eyes not overflowed / With trembling tears, he had imagined her / A marble statue. Love, before he knew, / Kindled; he gazed entranced; and overcome / By loveliness so exquisite, so rare, / Almost forgot to hover in the air...Reveal, I beg, your name and this land's name." Moreover, Perseus truly loves Andromeda upon saving her whereas Phineus saw Andromeda as a mere object for his social and political empowerment and advancement.

Perseus's faith in Minerva's revelation allows him to use the reflecting shield given to him to defeat Medusa. (Ovid's story of Perseus's slaying of Medusa is far less dramatic than Hollywood renderings, there isn't a fight at all as Perseus encounters the gorgon seductress asleep and turns her to stone without much struggle.) The hero then mounts Pegasus and soars into the skies and eventually comes across Andromeda "pinioned on a rock" as the sea monster Cetus approaches to devour her.

Again, it is Andromeda's face, her eyes, the windows into her soul, which capture the heroic heart of our hero. Rather than thinking her a statue he sees a human in distress and needing rescue. So Perseus ventures down from the heavens, a heaven-sent angel of deliverance, to rescue the sinless girl being punished for iniquity not her own but that of her mother. Perseus does battle with the sea monster, turns it to stone, and then frees Andromeda and begs her name—for, as mentioned, Perseus takes an interest in the soul and personality of Andromeda rather than her mere physical beauty.

Perseus's rescue of Andromeda endears him to her parents. Cepheus agrees that Perseus, not Phineus, should wed his daughter. This enrages Phineus whose plans of political advancement are now thwarted. During the wedding banquet of Perseus and Andromeda, Phineus and his henchmen storm the palace to slay the Perseus and steal Andromeda as a captive war bride. Ovid inserts into Cepheus's rebuke the reality of love against lust, love and personal empowerment, which serves as the marked contrast between Perseus and Phineus: "this / Your thanks for such great service? This the dower / You pay for her life saved? / It was not Perseus / Who took her from you, if you want the truth: / It was the Nereids and Neptune's wrath, / It was the horned Ammon, it was the sea-monster / Who came to feast upon my flesh and blood / You lost her then, then when her death was sure, / Unless her death indeed is what you want / And mean my grief to ease your cruel heart." Phineus, as revealed between the lines, cared not for Andromeda and only for himself and his ambitions; whether she lived or died on that rock was of little concern for him. By rescuing Andromeda, Cepheus's rebuke asserts, Perseus showed the magnanimity of his love to her. Phineus, enraged, hounds his men over the party but is defeated by Perseus whose love brings peace and order to the palace halls.

The story of Perseus and Andromeda is more hopeful, we might say, then many of the stories Ovid includes. Yet its theme is remarkably the same as most of the stories: the power of love in the midst of a world filled with carnage, death, and destruction. Where sorrow often reveals the heart of love in a love unconsummated (more on this in a moment), the love of Perseus and Andromeda reaches fruition in their marriage. They live a happy and joyful life together, blessed with many children who venture eastward and found new civilizations (per the story). So in the midst of all the skullduggery that surrounds the story of Perseus and Andromeda what do we find?

Love once again binds two flesh together as one. The love owed to the gods is rewarded in this instance, for it is Perseus's faith, and his piety, which separates him from Cassiopeia and Medusa. His genuine affection for the soul of Andromeda, rather than personal self-gain through political marriage, wins the heart of Andromeda in stark contrast to the naked vanity and ego of Phineus. The love Perseus and Andromeda share for each other is consummated in marriage and blessed with children, the highest good in much of ancient literature.

*

Yet not all the stories of love in Ovid's *Metamorphoses* have good endings. If Cadmus and Harmonia remained together in love even after being transformed into hideous snakes, and if the love of Perseus and Andromeda comes the closest to the Christian vision of divinization through love, what, then, do we make of all the stories of horror and sorrow that dot the landscape of Ovid's masterpiece?

Sorrow can be a testament of love. In fact, sorrow reveals to us the true totality of one's loving heart. The stories of Venus and Adonis, and Galatea and Acis, undoubtedly reveal the power of love through sorrow.

The story of Venus and Adonis is unique among the stories of intermingling between gods and humans in ancient myth and poetry. Most of the stories reveal capricious and lusty gods engaged in torment, torture, and outright violence toward the human captives of their eyes. This is not the case with Venus and Adonis. Jupiter may have swept down to steal and defile Europa, but Venus and Adonis share a far gentler, loving, and touching relationship.

As is customary, there is a dark and bleak backstory. The lust of Myrrha and Cinyras, for Myrrha has sex with her father and conceives Adonis through sin, is the origin of Adonis's birth into the cruel world of ever-changing tides of lust. For Adonis is a "wicked seed" and a child "conceived [in] crime." Yet as Adonis grows into manhood, an extremely handsome man at that, the gods take a new interest in this child of perdition.

Adonis is the apple in Venus's eye. So in love with Adonis is Venus that she is willing to "shun heaven too: to heaven she preferred / Adonis. Him she clung to, he was her / Constant companion." Adonis, too, is in love with Venus. Together they lay in each other's caressing arms with kisses delight that would make any god or mortal jealous just as Satan looked "with jealous leer malign / Eyed [Adam and Eve] askance, and to himself thus plained" upon seeing the love Adam and Eve shared with each other in the Garden of Eden. In their loving embrace Venus tells Adonis the story of Atalanta and Hippomenes before departing for Cyprus.

If Adonis was a child of sin, to which he cannot escape this fate and the law of incest must be punished, the tragedy of Venus and Adonis still reveals how love draws two together even in death and the memory of love lives on forever despite the gliding winds of time. Venus had warned Adonis not to be too bold and prideful on the hunt. This revelation of Venus to Adonis is discounted, for the young man acts with irreverence to the goddess's revelation which eventually leads him to his failed hunt wherein he is gorged by the boar and dies in the forest.

Despite Adonis's lack of living by the word of Venus, Venus is still drawn to his cries as she ventures to Cyprus. It is her love for Adonis which causes her to turn back, to rush to him in his final dying moments as he lay alone, blood spilling out of his groan, in the woods. Love unites lover and beloved even in death. While Venus curses the fates and is filled with sorrowful tears, her tears reveal her love for Adonis and how that love leads her to memorialize him for all eternity. Venus's tearful lament over Adonis's death establishes the cult of Adonia to commemorate his death. Likewise, her tears of love mingled with the blood of Adonis give birth to *Anemone* flowers, whose beauty reminds the world of the beauty of Adonis and stands as an everlasting and constantly blooming and reblooming reminder of the brief love they shared.

In sorrow Venus revealed her love for Adonis. And she left to the world, through the cult and festivals of Adonia, and the birth of the *Anemone* flower, an everlasting reminder of the love they shared. While this love could not be consummated to fruition, for many reasons—the two obvious pitfalls being the sinful lust of Myrrha and Cyranis from which Adonis was conceived and Adonis's own impiety of not heeding Venus's warning which was reinforced by the story of Atalanta and Hippomenes—the tears of Venus still show us the power of love in the midst of a world often beset by callousness, darkness, and violence.

*

So too, then, does the sorrowful lament of Galatea to Acis, crushed by the envious rage of the cyclops Polyphemus, reveal the poignancy of love in a tragic world.

Galatea was born from the lonely hands of the sculptor Pygmalion, who is brought to new life through the beauty of his marble-white statue turned real:

incumbensque toro dedit oscula visa tepere est;
admovet os iterum, manibus quoque pectora temptat:
temptatum mollescit ebur positoque rigore
subsidit digitis ceditque.

(Where she lay he kissed her, and she seemed warm to the touch,
so kissing her again and caressing her breasts,
the ivory grew soft in his fingers
and its hardness vanished into flesh.) [My translation]

With Pygmalion deceased, Galatea is free to roam the world where she is beset by the lust of the beast Polyphemus. Caught between the monster's predations and his "wild urge to kill" and the gentle love of Acis. Like Venus and Adonis, this story of the love between mortal and divine is free of the usual violent passions of the divine encroaching on the realm of human mortals. Like Venus and Adonis, the gentle love between mortal and divine cannot be consummated.

Yet the love shared between Acis and Galatea is touching and warming. It reveals their personalities. We learn something about the lovers in their fleeting moments together. It is not mere body heat that draws the two ill-fated lovers together. Personality draws them together as one. It is a love that is pure, a love that springs with joy and life—a purity and joy that makes Polyphemus rage with jealousy.

Here, Ovid reflects on the tragedy of love triangles. The rage that a scorned lover feels (Polyphemus) is what compels him to violent action. If he cannot have the love of Galatea no one can. Ovid, here, is remarkably modern in his outlook. The world of love is often messy as we know today. While some loves do consummate themselves in blissful happiness (as we saw with Perseus and Andromeda), other loves are beset by petty and violent rivalries and jealousies that lead to heartbreak and tragedy.

Polyphemus's lament reveals the emptiness of jealously, the envy that leads to violence: "I'll gauge his living guts, I'll rend his limbs / And strew them in the fields and in the sea." Looking upon the star-crossed lovers, Polyphemus springs into action. He violently storms down upon them, startling Galatea who flees into the sea leaving Acis alone to flee for his life. Acis cries out as he runs for his life, "Help, Galatea! Father, mother, help!" But there is no one to help poor Acis. Polyphemus lifts up a boulder and hurls it at Acis, crushing him, his blood spilling out over the fields. The murderous cyclops retreats to his cave, satisfied in the deadly deed done.

Galatea returns after Polyphemus has retreated to his blood-soaked cave. She stares, tears flowing, at the crushed body and spewing blood of her lover. But the gods and fates take pity on Galatea's tears. With permission from heaven, Galatea turns Acis's flowing blood into a river of life. The Jaci, in Sicily, is the river that bears Acis's blood transformed into an everlasting spring of love and life as the final farewell Galatea could give her lover.

In this story, Acis overcomes death through metamorphosis by love. The love that he shared with Galatea empowers Galatea to bring about his final transformation into a river of life that stands to memorialize the brief love the two shared. Rather than sink into the dust of the ground to be forgotten forever, Acis's blood is transformed into a beautiful spring of life that outlives Polyphemus. Once more we see in this tragic story how sorrowful tears reveal the spirit of love and how that love can overcome the tragedy of death.

Not all the stories that Ovid recounts necessarily have love as their central focus. Yet many do. And the stories capture Pythagoras's declaration that the soul remains constant amid the flux of life. Souls are united in love and that unity in love—whether as transformed snakes, blessed couples, or sorrowful lovers who witnessed their beloved die for all the reasons we ourselves are accustomed to (pride, vanity, foolishness, sin, jealousy, etc.)—never dies despite the death and tragedy that surrounds it.

I would also like to point out that in these stories, especially the sorrowful tales of death, that the final apotheosis of love takes us back to the imagery of gardens of love and life. We call these loving idylls by various names: Arcadia, Elysia, Eden. For these images of blossoming flowers and flowing rivers evoke a serenity of love beneath the sun and stars that still our restless hearts and bring us that peace amid the crushing and torrential winds of the cosmos. The cosmos may be dark, but Ovid's *Metamorphoses* remind us that there is intense beauty in this often cruel and dark world we inhabit. And that beauty is found in love, whether it is a love that brings joy or a love that brings sorrow—for even in sorrow we find the totality of the love that moves us to tears. As the Victorian poet Robert Browning Hamilton wrote:

I walked a mile with Pleasure;
She chatted all the way;
But left me none the wiser
For all she had to say.

I walked a mile with Sorrow;
And ne'er a word said she;
But, oh! The things I learned from her,
When Sorrow walked with me.

After chronicling these stories for us, and before Ovid inserts himself as the poet who will live on for eternity because of the truth "stablished by poetic prophecy," he gives final stage to Pythagoras.

It is interesting that Pythagoras takes center stage. Perhaps Ovid was himself a disciple of Pythagoras's doctrines. While we eventually yield to the unrelenting assault of the sea of time, Pythagoras says that our souls "Are still the same for ever" even if we "adopt / In their migrations ever-varying forms." But these varying forms that our souls adopt are still moved by that spirit of love: whether we be snakes, flowers, or rivers. Love is the pulsating soul that gives all things life.

If death be our fate as mortality must invariably end in death, what lives on? What is eternal? Love is eternal. When we look at trees, animals, and nature itself, we are to be reminded by the love that made the beauty of the world possible. That is Ovid's message and why Ovid can, confidently, assert that "[He] shall live" forever because of the "truth" "stablished by poetic prophecy" he poetically sang of. That truth is nothing short of the love that unites this disparate cosmos together.

Despite all the metamorphoses we witness, despite all the darkness and bloodshed our eyes often behold, despite the failures and frequent inability to consummate the love that we do seek, the constant spirit that governs Ovid's *Metamorphoses* is love: whether it be blessed, redemptive, or tragic. And that is why Ovid remains so powerful and relevant despite the violence and sexual predation that often accompanies his stories. We might say that he saw the world we are waking up to today. But rather than despair, we too should share is poetic truth that love can unite even death, and may, just may, in rare circumstances (like with Perseus and Andromeda) end in the felicity beside the flowers and streams of life we all desire. Reading Ovid is indeed a delight, a pleasure, especially once we know what he was singing about.

This essay was first published by *Merion West*, 11 November 2021.

Chapter 14

The Odyssey of Saint Augustine

In 430 AD, with the Vandals laying siege to the city of Hippo, Augustine of Hippo died with Count Boniface by his side. The Roman general was once a good friend of the bishop's but mismanagement of the Vandal invasion of North Africa brought a rupture in their friendship. Having retreated inside the city, Augustine and Boniface were reconciled as the Vandals laid siege. Two years later, Boniface died from wounds he suffered fighting Flavius Aetius near Rimini. It is fitting, however, that the great saint of North Africa—the "bishop of all North African writers" as Albert Camus would call him—died surrounded by his friends. For it brought full circle another famous death in Augustine's early life: the death of his mother, Saint Monica, and the love that this story told about Augustine's own understanding of love as the *appetitus inveniendi* of life itself.

Confessions is arguably Augustine's best-known work. What began as a response to Christological controversies in schismatic Christian communities in North Africa over the interpretation of Genesis 1 sprawled into a pseudo-autobiographical confession that made Augustine relatable and literarily immortal; as the great Henry Chadwick wrote, "as a literary figure [Augustine] must rank as one of the most remarkable writers of his age." As we know, young Augustine reflects on his life of sin, his life of being indoctrinated in a perverse Roman educational system that extolled selfishness and social climbing ("glory"), and his struggles in Carthage, Milan, and beyond.

Augustine, however, never abandoned his Virgilian pretensions and love of the great Roman epicist and poet whom he quoted more than Plato (which is oft forgotten in the historically inaccurate statement that Augustine "baptized" Plato; Augustine spoke highly of Plato in some places, but Plato ranked beneath even the Hebrew Prophets of Scripture and Virgil and Cicero in Augustine's voluminous writings). Just as Virgil offered poetic odyssey, Augustine emulated Virgil in the composition of his autobiographical section of the *Confessions*. That, perhaps, is the grandest achievement of Augustine's classic and why it remains such a deeply moving and enduring work. We find ourselves in Augustine: our hope, our desire, our journey; per Chadwick once again, "Augustine's story of his quest is all his own, and yet is simultaneously (and evidently consciously) intended to be a portrait of Everyman."

When Augustine mused who he was: *mihi quaestio factus sum* (who am I, or literally: I have become a question to myself), we reach the fullest crystallization of Augustine's interior odyssey. But Augustine's interior pilgrimage is not divorced from his physical pilgrimage he undertakes in the *Confessions*. Like Aeneas, his poetic idol crafted by his beloved poet, Augustine's spiritual journey is accompanied by a physical sojourn across the Mediterranean.

Reading the *Confessions* makes clear Augustine knew Virgil well. Perhaps too well. He even laments that he learned to weep for Dido more than his own depraved state of being. If Dante had a man crush on Virgil, Dante was merely following the footsteps of Augustine who had the first Christian man crush on Rome's most sublime poet.

Indeed, it can be argued that Augustine modeled his own journey in the *Confessions* after Aeneas's journey in the *Aeneid*. We have an exile driven to Carthage, from Carthage that exile manages to find his way to Rome where he experiences a conversion of grace and happiness through a vision halfway through the work just as Aeneas receives his *theoria* in the underworld halfway through the *Aeneid*. The exile now becomes a member, more intimately, of a community and becomes a warrior for love just as Aeneas becomes the warrior of love for his community of exilic Trojans as war in Italy commences for the future of civilization. From a "region of destitution" Augustine journeys to a place of "inexhaustible abundance" which echoes the very journey of Aeneas out of a city of destitution to a peninsula of Arcadian fragrance and abundance:

> *Intersea videt Aeneas in valle reducta seclusum nemus et virgulta sonantia silvae Lethaeumque, domos placidas qui praenatat, amnem. hunc cicum innumerae gentes populique volabant; ac velut in pratis ubi apes aestate serena floribus insidunt variis et candida circum lilia funduntur, strepit omnis murmure campus.*

> (Meanwhile in a quiet valley, Aeneas sees a secluded grove and roaring forest thickets and the river of Lethe rippling past many peaceful homes. In the valley danced innumerable peoples and tribes. Out in the

meadows, with the blue skies of summer shining overhead, bees land and feast on many hued blossoms and stream round lustrous flowers and lilies, and all the green pastures murmur with the buzzing and humming of life.) [My translation.]

That Region of Destitution

Augustine's restless heart moves him to a place of extreme restlessness. As Augustine enters Carthage to become a professor of rhetoric as a teenager, he reminisces on the hissing and bubbling cauldron that he finds himself in. And far from rejecting the temptations of his imaginative Babylon, Augustine openly indulges his passion in that crackling frying pan of illicit loves. Describing Carthage, Augustine bluntly states that it is a "region of destitution."

What is unique about Augustine's description of Carthage is how he pairs the physical lusts and destitution of the city with his own spiritual lusts and destitution. The spiritual is never separated from the carnal. Carthage is a godless place. A new Babylon, Augustine implies, to tempt the godly into the infernal fires while masking this pain with the false pleasures of fleeting ecstasy. (We must never forget that this is the same reality Carthage offers Aeneas when he arrives in Carthage.)

Over the course of the *Confessions*, we witness the progressive apotheosis of Augustine. While we remember his visions in Milan, his Neoplatonic ascent and crash, and then his famous weeping scene of conversion in the gardens of Milan when hearing the voice of the Christ Child speaking to him: *Tolle Lege, Tolle Lege* (take up and read, take up and read). What we forget, however, is that Augustine tries to climb to God while in Carthage but fails. And he fails miserably—which is why we probably forget it. For Augustine doesn't tell us of any vision of God he had, he only tells us of his abysmal failures to ascend to God.

Augustine dug himself a pit of destruction while in Carthage. Now trying to climb out, he weeps over his inability: "Despite my frequent efforts to climb out of it, I was the more heavily plunged back into the filth and wallowed in it." In this deep mire of darkness and falsity, Augustine has enslaved himself from God's blessedness and love that he nonetheless seeks. Moreover, while Monica has dreamt about Augustine (and has talked to Augustine about her dreams and her prayers for her son), Augustine is otherwise alone and alienated in Carthage. He has contacts with the Manicheans. He has sex with prostitutes. But all of this only serves to dig Augustine's ditch even deeper. Thus, when he attempts to "climb out of it" he only manages to plunge himself "back into the filth" and "wallow in it." As Augustine also writes, "I tried to approach you, but you pushed me away so that I should taste death, for you resist the proud."

Augustine's language in Carthage is deeply carnal and physical befitting the physical destitution that the city represents in his rhetorical composition. Thus we get the infamous physical imagery of Augustine stealing from the pear tree, feeding the fruit to a pig, wallowing in the hissing and crackling oil of his lusts, and plunging into the filth of the hole he dug for himself. Tears flow from his eyes. His mother also weeps for him. In this destitute and godless place, Augustine is himself destitute and godless. His spiritual emptiness is tethered to the emptiness of Carthage. Thus Augustine—like Aeneas—must flee Carthage to a godlier place: Italy.

From Augustine's own language, he cannot approach God while in Carthage. As a godless place, Carthage is no region to approach the God of abundance and heavenly fragrance. As I've said about this remarkable imagery and language constructed by Augustine, "[T]hese failed early attempts at climbing the ladder to God fail when he is in that province of barren destitution. Devoid of truth, wallowing in spiritual darkness, and living a life according to the wicked will, Augustine's attempt to ascend to God are not only held back because of his spiritual state, they are held back because of the physical place he is sinning in. The emptiness of Carthage leads to empty attempts to ascend whereby he falls back into the crackling and burning frying pan of his illicit loves. Carthage is not just a spiritual barrier but also a physical barrier to his journey with God." So break free from that physical barrier which doubles as a spiritual barrier Augustine must.

"I Found Myself Far From You"

Following Augustine's stint in Carthage, he makes use of his networking to meet with imperial officials in Rome. He then journeys to Milan, the city where the great Catholic bishop and priest Saint Ambrose resides. Between the pages, however, Augustine's flight from Carthage is to escape a woman: his mother. Readers of Virgil, of course, will find echoes of Aeneas's flight from Carthage to escape a woman: Queen Dido.

While in Milan Augustine experiences his first immortal vision, his glimpsing of the Beatific Vision as he slowly sheds his Manicheanism and now finds himself in a more wholesome place than Carthage. Italy is not that region of barren destitution as Carthage was. On the contrary, it is place teaming with life: gardens, trees, and, of course, godly men. It is also the place where Augustine sheds his wrongful thinking and abundant sinning which acts as a preparation for his journey to God.

The seventh book of the *Confessions* contain two infamous episodes in the work: a discourse on the philosophy of good and evil and the Neoplatonic vision which ends with Augustine crashing spectacularly back to earth having just glimpsed a mystical *theoria*. Interestingly, the movement to Augustine's encounter with God begins because he picked up some "books of the Platonists" which allowed him to free himself of his Manichaean thinking.

All philosophy and theology students are undoubtedly familiar with Augustine's treatment of evil here. He argues that there is nothing intrinsically evil, for if there was something intrinsically evil that would jeopardize the benevolence of God. Augustine's philosophy of evil is also a shielded theodicy protecting God from he would consider sacrilege and blasphemy. He goes on to argue that evil is a privation of nature, a depreciation of that which is inherently good by virtue of its created status. Evil, thus, is located in an act of will—action—rather than anything natural or inherent.

What is often missed in Augustine's rumination on evil is how will manifests evil: lack of understanding.

The entirety of the *Confessions* is a longwinded poetic treatise on the nature of truth. Augustine argues that humans are made for truth and love (since God is Truth and Love and humans are made in the image of God this logically follows). Where we sin, or fall short, is in our misapprehension of truth and love—a misunderstanding that distorts the goodness that does, in fact, drive human desire. By improperly understanding nature, Augustine is arguing, our will engages in evil actions because misunderstanding is the precondition to the will privating goodness in the natural world. Properly speaking, one's *logos* must be unified with one's *voluntas*.

Only after having learned this truth from the Platonists can Augustine free himself from the shackles of Manichean misunderstanding which prevented him from ascending to God in Carthage. Augustine employs a rhetorical and intellectual—indeed, poetic—skill in building the momentum toward his first, though distant, glimpse of the Godhead. Augustine must first begin to understand before he can proceed to see, reason and will are united at last to offer him something more than the emptiness which has otherwise dominated his life: "I entered and with my soul's eye, such as it was, saw above that same eye of my soul the immutable light higher than my mind—not the light of every day, obvious to anyone, nor a larger version of the same kind which would, as it were, have given out a much brighter light and filled everything with its magnitude."

Augustine glimpses the sublime and the beautiful, the radiance of God—Christ—in his mystic ascent begotten from his encounter with the Platonist books. Yet Augustine does not yet know Christ and His name, thus, he is still rebuffed. Augustine, here, implies that Platonist theology and mysticism contains the seeds of divine truth, but lacking divine revelation it is not capable of actually seeing Christ and bringing one's soul into paradise. Having glimpsed paradise, Augustine nevertheless falls back to earth in a weeping wreck: "I found myself far from you 'in a region of dissimilarity,' and heard as it were your voice from on high: 'I am the food of the fully grown; grow and you will feed on me.'"

By now we know Augustine is, and still remains, a proud human being. However, unlike the stuffed-up pride of the Platonists (like Porphyry, his great Platonic interlocutor he self-cultivated in *The City of God*) who would have patted themselves on the back for such a vision, Augustine finally embraces a moment of humility—dwelling not on how close he came to God but how far he found himself from God. "I found myself far from you," Augustine laments. (Though we might detect a trace of hidden pride in Augustine being satisfied with himself in acknowledging how far away he was.)

But this vision of the mind, which is the soul, is only possible because Augustine has freed his mind from the pollution of Manichaean thought and the crud of Carthaginian mud. Again, it is important for the reader to recognize that Augustine's odyssey is not merely spiritual and interior; it is physical and carnal. Augustine's glimpse of God comes not only after he has gained some spiritual and intellectual insight, it comes also in a place far removed from the hissing and crackling cauldrons and frying pans of Carthage.

Augustine has soared up Diotima's Ladder and found it lacking: "I sought a way to obtain strength enough to enjoy you; but I did not find it until I embraced 'the mediator between God and man, the man Christ Jesus, who is above all things, God blessed for ever…To possess my God, the humble Jesus, I was not yet humble enough." As fruitful as the Platonist books were in setting Augustine free, they were not enough to save Augustine. No, the books of Plato and Plotinus may point you in the right direction but it will take the voice of Christ in the form of a babe to finally push Augustine across the finish line in crushing humility. (Halfway through the work, in following the tradition of Virgilian poetry, and with the presence of another, Augustine finally receives his revelation of new life that will drive him toward this epic's conclusion.)

"Step By Step We Climbed"

Augustine's final vision occurs after his conversion in the gardens of Milan when the voice of Christ in the form of an infant cries out to him: *Tolle Lege, Tolle Lege*. Augustine listens, at last, and begins reading the Epistle of Saint Paul to the Romans. Augustine has finally swallowed the medicine of the soul he has long sought. En route back to North Africa, with Monica once again by his side (along with his friends, most notably Alypius), Augustine and Monica are no longer separated (by the phantasmagoria of dreams or the literal running away from his momma). They are, at last, together and at peace.

Let us briefly return to another point of compositional brilliance on the part of the bishop of Hippo. In Carthage, he was alone. Even in Milan, he was alone. Augustine's loneliness and emptiness are directly tied to his spiritual alienation.

Humans, being made in love for love, are not meant to be alone. Truly, "it is not good for man to be alone." Augustine, who has thus far been alone, is now surrounded by the company of friends and loved ones. Love, at long last, has taken hold of Augustine. For the first time in the *Confessions* Augustine is not alone or surrounded by the crowd and hissing cauldrons of lust that manifest, in their raucousness, the isolation that Augustine was in despite the seeming appearance of others around him. (Take, for example, Augustine's stealing of the pear/fig with friends; when he confesses his sin, he is alone because he was always alone.)

Moreover, in escaping Thagaste for Carthage, and Carthage for Rome, Augustine was fleeing from the persistent presence of Monica. Between the lines, although Augustine was an undeniable momma's boy, he felt suffocated by her tears, prayers, and dreams. Augustine's flight to ruin, celebrity, and conversion were also motivated by his want to free himself from the presence of his mother. Yet Monica persists in her love for Augustine and tracks him down in Italy and is with him as they journey together to Ostia in hope to return to North Africa.

There, however, Monica falls ill. The mother that was always praying for Augustine (and beside Augustine) was a true conduit of love. Augustine, at long last, recognizes this. No longer alone, Augustine recounts his most brilliant vision in his mother's arms:

The conversation led us towards the conclusion that the pleasure of the bodily sense, however delightful in the radiant light of this physical world, is seen by comparison with the life of eternity to not even be worth consideration. Our minds were lifted up by an ardent affection towards eternal being itself. Step by step we climbed beyond all corporeal objects and the heaven itself, where sun, moon, and stars shed light on the earth. We ascended even further by internal reflection and dialogue and wonder at your works, and we entered into our own minds. We moved up beyond them so as to attain to the region of inexhaustible abundance where you feed Israel eternally with truth for food. There life is the wisdom by which all creatures come into being, both things which were and which will be. But wisdom itself is not brought into being but is as it was and always will be. Furthermore, in this wisdom there is no past and future, but only being, since it is eternal... And while we talked and panted after it, we touched it in some small degree by a moment of concentration of the heart. And we sighed and left behind us the 'firstfruits of the Spirit' bound to that higher world, as we returned to the noise of our human speech where a sentence has both a beginning and an ending.

The odyssey of love has finally triumphed. In love, with another—his mother, no less, who had dreamt of their being together—Augustine finally beholds that Love which had eluded him his whole life. The ascent to have a vision of the Love that is the Beatific Vision occurs only because Augustine has finally come to understand what love is.

In *De Trinitate*, Augustine defined the Trinity as a relations of love. In his voluminous other writings, though entailed and implied throughout the *Confessions*, he also had much to say on friendship. Friendship and family, Augustine would come to argue, are the first instantiations of the love of the Trinity in our life. God is love. Therefore, Augustine would eventually conclude love is God. And love is first nurtured with our family and our friends, the two pillars of love in the world that most intimately reflect the love of the Godhead.

It is here, in Ostia, we witness the "firstfruit of the Spirit" of love that Augustine had long sought. He had "wanted to love and be loved." In the arms of his mother he ascends with her and her with him to the realm of "inexhaustible abundance," the inexhaustible abundance of Love itself. This is an odyssey we do not take alone. The journey to Love is a pilgrimage that always entails others. "It is not good for man to be alone." The very image of God, the image of love, is not merely beheld by Augustine and Monica, they themselves have become incarnate manifestations of the *imago Dei* in the love they shared in that final moment.

From Loneliness to Love

Augustine's *Confessions* begins in loneliness and lust but ends in fellowship and love. The alienated lust that so grips Augustine's heart like crackling oil in a frying pan becomes a still calm spirit producing the fruit of serenity. Love flows freely between Augustine and Monica, and between Augustine and his friends (principally Alypius) at the conclusion of the autobiographical portion of the *Confessions* in a way heretofore unseen in the narrative.

Confessions is a book of images. And it concludes, both in the autobiography and the spiritual commentary (Book XIII) with grand imagery. What is more loving, and beautiful, than the flourishing of human love—especially between a mother and son—which is, itself, a human manifestation of the Divine Love that Dante would later say "moves the sun and the other stars."

The endurance of Augustine is that we, like him, seek love and desire to be loved. Like Augustine, we too have dug ourselves holes, tried to ascend, persisted in stubborn loneliness, and only climbed out with the help of a face out of whose smile flows the love that we have always sought. Love truly does "move the sun and the other stars." Dante knew his Augustine. And it was in that loving fellowship that Augustine, like Aeneas, finally saw Arcadia and the valley of life and love eternal with the company of others, not alone or alienated like in Carthage, not in a valley of tears, but a valley teeming with life and the dancing laughter of all creation.

This essay was first published by *VoegelinView*, 20 December 2021.

Chapter 15

Augustine's *City of God*:
The First Culture War

Love is the central feature of Augustine's writings. All humans, irrespective of their state of grace, Augustine argued, desire to love and be loved. The role of love has a direct impact upon the political in Augustine's political theology since humans are political animals defined by their loves. What people love will become the aim of politics and society.

The Origin of Christian Criticism

The city of man, founded on its love of self, inevitably exhausts itself in its lust for domination and an ethos of coercive domination in (false) hope to satisfy the self. The city of man, therefore, is that "city which aims at domination, which holds nations in enslavement, but is itself dominated by that very lust of domination." The city of God, by contrast, rooted in its love of God, promotes cooperation and a hopeful restoration of pre-Fall harmony. As he charts out the two cities in *The City of God*, it becomes clear that Augustine's theology is also the first systematic form of cultural critique aimed at exposing the empty ideology and propaganda of *altae moenia Romae*.

This should not be surprising. Many scholars also recognize the critical project of Augustine's work. Ernest Fortin notes that the aim of Augustine's critique was to "unmask [the pagan political system's] vices." Peter Brown, likewise, argues that part of *The City of God* was written to critically examine the hypnotizing "myth of Rome." By analyzing, deconstructing, and unmasking the vices of pagan Rome, Augustine's political theology is primarily one of critique. Augustine's political theology is also deeply dialectical and imaginative: It is based on images of contrast.

Augustine makes known that the city of man is characterized by its desire to satisfy its disordered passions. The city of man "was created by love of self reaching the point of contempt of God." To understand the city of man, of which all humans are transient citizens, we must ask the question *quid sit homo*: what is man?

According to Christianity's doctrine of creation, *creatio ex nihilo*, the proper understanding of humanity is that humanity ultimately came from nothing. Humanity is only truly human when clothed in grace, but the fall of man has stripped man of his grace and he is now "naked" as Augustine explained. Apart from God, "naked of grace," man is nothing—man is, to put it mildly, a domineering brute captured by lust which is the privation of love.

To love only the self is to love what one is apart from God—namely, the naked and domineering brute who has no grace covering him. Therefore, the love of self is the love of nothing because it rejects enjoying God and, in the process, rejects self-emptying love and goodness which serves as the groundwork for the harmonious unity of humanity with each other, and with creation, prior to the Fall. Following the Augustinian maxim of becoming what one loves, it is also true that the political comes to promote what its citizenry desires. Culture and politics subsequently inculcate what its citizens love through its apparatuses, institutions, and other structural systems creating a mass society united in such a love. Based on his own experience as a citizen, Augustine most poignantly critiques Roman power and institutional structures which promote and inculcate the love of nothingness.

Deconstructing the Myth of Rome

Augustine recounts his time being formed by the conventions and institutions of Roman society and remarks as to what kind of human Roman institutions and systems had made him. The educational apparatus of the late Western Roman Empire inculcated the love of self into Augustine. As he explains in *Confessions*, he would lie, cheat, and engage in flattery to win the praises of others who honored him a role model and exemplary student. He stole from his parents to barter and possess the toys of his classmates. The rhetorician that he was, Augustine put his command of speech in the service of slavery rather than truth—to get what he wanted and therefore control others in the process. His actions to win the praise of others was symptomatic of his self-love and self-seeking glory that Roman education instilled into him, and he also acknowledged that the educational system—of which system he was upheld as a sterling exemplar—led him astray from God.

In reading Virgil's *Aeneid* and appreciating the deep beauty therein, Augustine learned to weep for Dido and her surrender to the sword all the while he sank lower and lower in his own pit of despair. Jupiter too, his teachers informed him, would punish the wicked; yet, Jupiter constantly engaged in immoral acts himself. From this picture Augustine understood that Roman education was shifting the blame of wickedness to the gods—freeing humans to engage in their base actions. (Here, Augustine begins a long tradition in Christian theology that seeks to demonstrate God as free from evil; evil is a product of human free will and not God's decrees.) In this way the love of self and the self's desires to remain inward rather than to serve others was justified through the texts and stories that he learned.

Far from the humanistic education that Cicero advocated, Roman education, whose moral collapse Cicero identified as the cause of the downfall of the Roman republic and its transition into empire, extolled wickedness and self-centeredness as the highest aspiration. Because Roman society loved only the self, Roman society ultimately loved nothing, and it aspired to nothing and promoted this aspiration to its future generations. And the individual who best embodied this love of nothingness was hailed as a great role model to others.

From Augustine's point of view, Jupiter, then, is not punishing the wicked for transgressions but punished simply out of a display of his own power and egotistical desires. Jupiter does what Jupiter does because he has the power to do so; moral guidance or the moral law is not a factor in Jupiter's activities. The Roman Empire demonstrates this reality of domineering exploitation by modelling itself on *Jupiter Invictus Rex Caelis*.

This love of self, Augustine charged, was the reason for the existence of the Roman pantheon. The civic religion of Rome, like its educational system, promoted the love of self, acting on which individuals could win flattery of the people and the approval of the gods. The civic cults only furthered the promotion of self-flattery and egotism above any higher truths or moral rectitude.

As Augustine subsequently mused, if truth or moral fortitude was the aim of Rome, as its defenders often claimed, then why was there not a single shrine to Plato? The Roman gods embodied immorality and thereby sanctioned wicked imitation of the gods. The Roman people became puppets of (immoral) gods. What was most disconcerting for Augustine was that he was formed and instructed to be one of those immoral puppets, and joyfully and willingly embraced that lifestyle for much of his early, pre-conversion life.

One of the constant themes of Roman inculturation, beyond its brutality, was the celebration of death. The Homeric epics, Virgil's *Aeneid*, and the stories of Jupiter smiting the immoral with thunderbolts (all the while he engaged in immoral activities himself) all celebrate death and destruction in some manner—a manifestation of humanity's self-destructive impulses. Perhaps the most tragic example of this praising of nothingness (death) was the rape and suicide of Lucretia whose story was one of the most important founding myths of the Roman people. According to Rome's mythology, Lucretia's rape by one of Tarquin's sons and her subsequent suicide awakened the slumbering sentiments of the Roman people to the tyrannical monarchy and spurred them to overthrow the king. Thus, Lucretia was revered as a virtuous heroine who played a role in the founding of the Roman republic in the place of tyranny.

Leading up to Lucretia's suicide, Augustine began his commentary on suicide more broadly as a topic. Therein he concluded that suicide is not a viable option for dealing with trauma and the absurdities of life. Suicide is the result of fear of punishment, shame, or guilt. Augustine was perplexed by the dilemma in which Lucretia found herself: Was she chaste or had she committed adultery? As he poignantly asked, "If she is adulterous, why is she praised? If chaste, why was she put to death?"

For Augustine, the rape and suicide of Lucretia highlighted the moral depravity of Roman society, its institutions, and its aims. Lucretia had done nothing wrong. And yet, she ultimately decided to end her life. As Augustine concluded, it was the feeling of shame from defilement fostered by Roman society which caused her to commit suicide. Her blood was as much on the hands of the Romans as it was on Tarquin's son. Shame, the product of Roman culture, killed her.

The burden of shame of no longer being able to live up to the Roman ideal purity pushed her to her death. As Augustine tragically noted, Roman society had inculcated into her a drive of self-pride and honor, and when it was ripped away from her because of "another's foul deed committed *on* her, even though not *with* her, and as a Roman woman, excessively eager for honour, she was afraid that she should be thought, if she lived, to have willingly endured what, when she lived, she had violently suffered." Romans held up Lucretia as a paragon of virtue only because she killed herself out of guilt and shame.

The guilt Lucretia felt was caused by the loss of self-love, pride, and purity which Roman society praised so highly. As St. Thomas Aquinas later noted, in a hopeless society people die to avoid shame. To avoid the shame of having lost her purity, Lucretia had no hope and consequently chose death. Had she not killed herself, Augustine's reflection implies, she would have been mocked and scorned by the same Romans who eventually celebrated her.

The irony of the story is that it encapsulated the Roman infatuation with power and death and, through the propaganda machinery of Roman education and embodied ethos, subsequently turned it into one of "virtue" and "sacrifice." Lucretia had become the sacred outcast, though through no fault of her own, and paid the ultimate price for her defilement at the hands of another. She was innocent of the crimes which had caused her to choose death over life, but, moreover, she was a victim of social sin and structural pressure.

When dignity was stripped from her, having become objectified by Tarquin's son, Lucretia had nothing left to live for and so thrust the sword into her heart with Roman society cheering her every step of the way. In Lucretia's story we see the most poignant reflection of Augustine's understanding of the *libido dominandi*, the turning of a subject person into an object of predatory control.

Augustine reads the rape of Lucretia as a damning indictment against social sin, structural power, and egotistical culture which culminated in the tragedy of Lucretia's suicide. What is made all the more egregious is how blind the Romans were to this reality, cloaking everything with the celebratory veil of virtue, only because it was not they who had suffered and died like Lucretia. In other words, better her than them. In Lucretia's story one sees that coercive domination hard at work through social forces as much as through institutional and systematic forces. It was only through Lucretia's death that she won the self-honor and self-praise Roman society aimed for—but as an objectified thing. The pressures of Roman society, that self-love inculcated through Roman "virtues" and social systems, pushed Lucretia out of society not because of her own deeds but by the foul deeds of another upon her, as Augustine so poignantly noted.

In Lucretia's story the ultimate self-reduction of the city of man based on the love of the self, and only the self, is manifested: Everyone becomes an object to be objectified in the sight of the beholder. Augustine openly acknowledges that this is what happened to him. In seeking love and happiness he sought after *something* to love. Therefore, it was only natural that he sought after things to satiate his desires. And so, Lucretia had become an object to be used by Tarquin's son and an object extolled by the Romans after her death.

Never once was there a trace of seeing other humans as images of God made in love for love. The love of self reduces itself to either objectifier (becoming an agent of coercive objectification) or objectified (becoming the passive object of objectification). Augustine saw the tragic irony of the fate of Lucretia: It was only in her objectification and subsequent death that she won the praises of the city of man. The love of self, inculcated and writ large, can only win praise by arriving at self-love's final end: death. Roman heroes, in Augustine's critique and reading, were only remembered for how they died or conquered others—never in how they loved and served others.

Likewise, Augustine doesn't spare the other great founding myth of Rome from critique: the story of Romulus and Remus. Augustine immediately recognized that the founding of Rome, like the founding of earthly cities in the Genesis account, stems from the sin of fratricide. Romulus murders his brother Remus out of lust for domination, which characterizes the city of man. Both sought the glory of Rome's founding for themselves.

This want for self-glory and self-honor led to the lust for domination, forming a competition between the two, which ended in murder. "For this is how Rome was founded, when Remus, as Roman history witnesses, was slain by his brother Romulus. The difference from the primal crime was that both brothers were citizens of the earthly city. Both sought glory of establishing the Roman state, but a joint foundation would not bring to each the glory that a single brother would enjoy." As Augustine also poignantly noted, the founding myth of Rome is not only one covered in the blood of fratricide but also internal division (and filial division at that). For the city of man cannot be united since love of self cannot bind people together: "Thus the quarrel that arose between Remus and Romulus demonstrated the division of the earthly city against itself."

Cicero's Folly

One can see in Augustine's critique of the city of man that the city of man became what the human heart desired: domination. The very machinery and institutional apparatus of the city subsequently embodied that ethos and perpetuated it in its many systems. The political was entirely organized on the principle of the love of self, leading to its debasement and self-destruction.

Augustine's city of man, rooted in the love of self, is what we might call a vile state, a base state, and despotic state wrapped altogether in one aimless, coercive, and domineering city. Augustine's reading of self-love in the city of man is that it must necessarily exhaust itself in the pursuit of power and it cannot be satiated until dominion is established over everything in the world. After all, the founding myths of Rome—Romulus and Remus, Aeneas, and Lucretia—all involve death and domination. And that other great story of Rome, the murder of Julius Caesar in the name of saving the Roman republic, was yet another repeat of the only thing Rome knew—that blood must be spilled for praise, honor, and liberty to be won.

The city of man, then, truly is the city "which aims at domination" (to try and satisfy the self). The love of self necessarily leads to a dissolved and dissipated body, itself a corrupted parody of the original condition of harmony, integrity, and mutual respect founded on common love (of God). That common love which binds together, rather than separates and divides, is a "love that is the whole-hearted and harmonious obedience of mutual affection." And so, it is in love that Augustine's criticism of Cicero is most properly brought to light. Cicero and Augustine both agree that a republic is based on the common good, but Augustine understood that common good is an extension of a common love; for the good is tied to love itself. Without a common love there is only division and the reduction of life to tyranny as Rome's history testified.

Cicero called the republic a republic only insofar that the populace was united in a common sense of right and wrong. Cicero even acknowledged the importance of morality in the foundation of the republic and that without that morality the morality ceased to exist in all but name. Yet Augustine questions as to whether this republic of Cicero's imagination ever existed at all. Cicero may have been a light in the darkness, but he was otherwise blind to the fact that political apparatus of Rome promoted the very opposite of what he claimed the republic embodied. Only from that common sense of right and wrong could justice be dispensed, but Augustine bleakly asserted such a republic never existed, even according to Cicero's own definition:

> For unjust human institutions are not to be called or supposed to be institutions of right, since even they themselves say that right is what has flowed from the fount of justice; as for the notion of justice commonly put forward by some misguided thinkers, that it is the 'the interest of the strongest,' they hold this to be a false conception... Therefore, where

there is no true justice there can be no 'association of men united by a common sense of right,' and therefore no people answering to the definition of Scipio, or Cicero.

Because Rome was organized on self-love, rather than a common love which consummated in recognition of subjects of love, it could never possess that shared community of right and wrong which comes only from love of God. Everyone would love his own vision of the good and seek to manifest it. Justice was therefore always centered on the self for the end of self-gain resulting in republics and kingdoms devolving into "criminal gangs." There was no healing and uniting dispensation of justice in Cicero's time, before Cicero's time, or after Cicero's time, precisely because the republic he so courageously defended was founded on "the love of self reaching to the point of contempt of God."

Since Cicero's republic was centered on self-love (and self-praise), its sense of right and wrong was relativized, and the justice, for which the republic stood, was incomplete and equally relativized. Because of the nature of relativism with regard to the justice of the Roman republic, which benefited those in power for self-aggrandizing ends, there was never a unity of "right and wrong." In *The City of God*, Augustine mostly critiques Cicero's blindness to the truth that the Roman Republic was an immoral entity predicated on domination and slavery; it was therefore "useless for Cicero to cry out against [immorality]" because the very republic he was eulogizing was a republic founded on the very immorality he was excoriating.

Partly because the city lives by the standard of falsity rather than of truth, the city of man descends into self-exhausting destruction. Since God is Truth itself, the city of man, in rejecting God, rejects Truth. Without truth there can be nothing to keep the city of man united. This is what Cicero ultimately failed to realize.

Cicero, ironically, spoke only to himself befitting of the reality of Rome's promotion of the love of self. Rome had no hope, as most brutally revealed in Lucretia's rape and suicide.

The politics of lust and domination drive the city of man to its extirpation. As Augustine then goes on to show, Rome's rise to greatness was predicated on its lust to control the world—not by any virtue of its own, as its apologists claimed. The haunting words of Virgil remind us of this reality: *genus unde Latinum Albanique patres atque altae moenia Romae* (then came the Latin race, the lords of Alba, and the high walls of mighty Rome).

The City of God and the Hope of the World

If the city of man stands for coercion and the lust for domination, what does the city of God embody than just "the love of God to the point of contempt of the self"? Augustine defines the Trinity as a relation of love, and if one saw and embodied love, one saw and embodied the Trinity. The consequence of Augustine's thought is the idea that the love of God is most purely manifested through the love of one's neighbor.

As Augustine recounted, how could have that city embodying the "honourable love of friends" started "if the life of the saints were not social"? Augustine's city of God does not flee from the many ills, wrongs, enmities, war, and other "undoubted evils" that exist, but directly engages with the world—love requires engagement rather than retreat. Augustine's political theology encourages a social life preoccupied with loving service, seeking justice, and the dispensation of that justice to individuals and parties that have been wronged by "grievous ills" and "criminal trials" which plague the city of man.

The love of others, on which the city of God is founded, is not a call to separation but a call to the shepherding and transforming of the earthly city in imitation of the heavenly. It is, in Reinhard Niebuhr's words, the call of moral man into immoral society and not the call of moral man to withdraw entirely from immoral society. In this manner Augustine, like Aristotle and Cicero before him, tacitly critiques the Cynic and Epicurean traditions which called for societal withdrawal. What use is love and virtue if one withdraws back into isolation? This retreat is, in some way, analogous to the denial of bearing one's cross and imitating Christ.

Just as the city of man embodied, reflected, and forcefully promoted the love of self, the city of God exists in dialectical opposition to that city run by criminal gangs and criminal trials; the city of God embodies, reflects, and compassionately promotes—through imitation—the love of God through the social lives of the saints. The city of God is *imitatio Christi* writ large: "The Heavenly City…serve[s] one another in love." After all, Christ's command to the disciples was to baptize the nations and not atomized and solitary individuals.

The city of God is social, and its love is social—the city of God is itself the embodiment of the whole of the Law, which Christ taught is loving God and neighbor. The love of God necessitates the love of neighbor, which has social implications and ramifications for life in the earthly city. The search for love and justice is grounded in one's family, but it does not remain situated with the family. This love eventually spreads outward to others.

It is fair, then, to assess that Augustine's city is founded not on the family, per se, but on love and justice in whose fostering the family plays an integral role. For without love there can be no family, so love comes first from which all else flows. In the city of man, lust comes first from which all else disintegrates. Augustine stands apart from Aristotle and Cicero who both identify the family as the cornerstone of civilization—Augustine's theology reveals something deeper than the family: Love (and more specifically, *Amor Dei*). Love is what gives birth to the family and where love is first nurtured; love precedes the family and therefore love is the first cornerstone of civilization (thus we see how a republic cannot come into being without a common love first).

The love of others is fully revealed in Augustine's recount of the Sack of Rome when Christians in the city sheltered pagan Romans in their hour of need: "The sacred places of the martyrs and the basilicas of the apostles bear witness to this, for in the sack of Rome they afforded shelter to fugitives, both Christian and pagan." In fleeing from the bloodlust and rampage of the Visigoths, Roman pagans suddenly found themselves being aided by the Christians whom they ridiculed.

The demand of the city of God, then, is the call to self-emptying. That "love of God to the point of contempt of the self" is the opposite of self-love and lust. This was seen most dramatically during the sack of Rome. During this tumultuous moment Christians did not discriminate against those whom they would shelter from the horrors of the slaughter outside the walls of their sanctuaries but truly embodied that ethos of self-emptying love even toward those whom they knew despised them at every level of their being.

We can conclude that Augustine is the strongest critic of social sin of the patristic period and remains one of the greatest critics of "immoral society" and what it does to individuals. Far from bleakly pessimistic, Augustine's political theology offers a glimpse of the city of love and the love of others which constitutes the pulsating heart of city of God. The city of God is not merely a distant city where souls go after death; it is the city in which living persons exhibit the love of others (rather than the love of self). That city will transit, or make passage, into the Heavenly City—but it has roots in this world passing into the next. The city of love and the relations of love in this world prefigure the City of Love to come, which St. Paul says is the true hope of

Christians and the only hope for the world. For this City of Love and Peace, which Augustine argues is the destination of the Christian, is also the city Homer and Virgil longed for.

In the first half of *The City of God* Augustine systematically lays bare the empty ideology of the city of man and the Roman *imperium* in a breathtaking counter-narrative that remains remarkably modern and relevant for today. Those blinded by their own imaginary Rome, like Cicero, fail to see the darkness that so governed the so-called "eternal city" challenging that other eternal city toward which Christians are pilgrimaging. But this is pitiable from Augustine's perspective. For in their blindness Augustine extends a hand of mercy and love to his critics; he extends his loving hand to those lost in the sea of domination by referencing Virgil and directing them to true city that will satiate their desires: "Now take possession of the Heavenly Country, for which you will have to endure but little hardship; and you will reign there in truth and love for ever."

This essay was first published by *The Imaginative Conservative*, 15 August 2020.

Afterword

In this selection of essays, I have gathered a concise pilgrimage through the principal classics of the Greco-Latin world that are widely known and often read in classical, or humanities-based, curriculums. The Victorian poet and literary critic Matthew Arnold wrote that art and literature contained "the best that has been thought and said" about the human condition. I concur. And "the best that has been thought and said" about the common human condition we have and share with our ancient forebears is contained in the patrimony of the Western literary tradition.

It is inarguable that love is the central theme of the great works. From Homer and his heirs, even to Plato, Plutarch, Plotinus and the Greek philosophers, to the Roman literary poets, to, of course, Augustine and the Christian theological tradition, love is the principal focus of the writings of the great artists who blazed the trail for us to look upon the good things the heavens hold. The vast array of considerations on love, from love bringing healing, to love bringing enmity and scorn, to love being construed as lust, all teach us the turbulent twists and turns of the human heart and soul in its search for love and its many failures to actualize it.

This book begins with Homer and the Greeks and ends with Saint Augustine of Hippo. The choice for ending with Augustine may be perplexing to some. Augustine was a Christian where all the others preceding him in this selection are not. Yet Augustine was the child of the classical tradition as any reader and scholar of Augustine knows. Augustine was immersed in the philosophical and literary traditions of Athens and Rome which formed his own mind and tugged and pulled on his own heart.

The decision to end with Augustine is appropriate on several accounts. Augustine's *Confessions* is treated as classical literature even in the non-religious world. From literature to philosophy, Augustine's *Confessions* generally marks the end of the classical tradition and begins the transition to the medieval world where Christianity is the dominant religion and outlook. Yet the *Confessions*, as I've attempted to show in its inclusion in this volume, still very much speaks to the classical heart and soul: that yearning for love and imitation of the grand epics of the Greco-Roman imagination.

Yet Augustine was much more than just the odd offspring of the Greco-Roman cultural and intellectual tradition. He is, arguably, one of the most important figures in Western cultural history. Thus the selection doesn't end with the *Confessions* but with the *City of God*. *The Confessions* may engage in cultural critique and criticism of the very wellspring from which Augustine drank and sprang from, but the *City of God* offers the penetrating critique and antidote to that tradition which Augustine was never fully nourished by. It is appropriate, in my mind, that after having examined the plethora of classical texts included in this volume that it ends with Augustine's appraisal of their shortcomings. However moving Homer, Aeschylus, and Virgil may be—and they certainly are—Augustine saw insufficiencies in them. We might go as far as to say Augustine wept with Homer, Aeschylus, and Virgil for not having been privy to the revelation of Christ. How close, yet how so far! Lastly, Augustine serves as the bridge connecting the emergent Christian world to the classical past of antiquity and how that living well does not need to be dried up but can receive new life by Love itself.

It is, therefore, from Augustine's eyes that we can see the beauty, goodness, and truth contained in the classical authors even if but in shadowy form. Their concern for love, how love brings healing and reconciliation, how the rejection of love leads to suffering and misery, how unchecked passion can lead to lust and hatred, ring true for us today as it did for listeners of readers of antiquity. Far from irrelevance, the classics have enduring relevance precisely because they are works dealing with the human heart and soul. We are the heirs of the classical tradition and what they wrestled with and we wrestle with the same issues they sang about.

In our deracinated cultural world today, the classics need safeguarding by true guardians of culture who will build up the beauty, goodness, and truth contained in the mighty works of Homer, the poets and playwrights and Greece and Rome, and even the patristic fathers who seem so distant to us moderns removed many centuries from them. It is my hope that this selection of reflections on the classics brings out the wisdom, truth, and above all, love, that is the heart of the classical tradition. We forsake this great wellspring at our own peril. So to you, dear reader, I say read on! Read on to the stars. *Per aspera ad astra.*

Bibliography

As this is a collection of essays written in the popular style, I have opted to include a bibliography of the versions of the works quoted from in the various essays. In doing so I have chosen popular editions that are widely accessible and likely versions read in classical curriculum schools and classrooms. They do not necessarily represent my endorsement of a translation. In lieu of Robert Fagles's more contemporary translations of Homer, I also recommend the slightly more archaic, but poetically beautiful, translations by Richmond Lattimore.

Aeschylus. *The Oresteia*. Translated by Robert Fagles. New York: Penguin, 1979.

Aristophanes. *Frogs and Other Plays*. Translated by David Barrett. New York: Penguin, 2007.

Aristophanes. *Lysistrata and Other Plays*. Translated by Alan Sommerstein. New York: Penguin, 2002.

Augustine. *The City of God*. Translated by Marcus Dods. New York: Modern Library, 2000.

Augustine. *Confessions*. Translated by Marcus Dods. New York: Oxford University Press, 2008.

Catullus. *The Poems of Catullus*. Translated by Daisy Dunn. London: William Collins, 2016.

Euripides. *The Trojan Women and Other Plays*. Translated by James Morwood. New York: Oxford University Press, 2008.

Euripides. *Ten Plays*. Translated by Paul Roche. New York: Signet, 1998.

Herodotus. *The Histories*. Translated by Aubrey de Sélincourt. New York: Penguin, 2003.

Hesiod. *Theogony and Works and Days*. Translated by M.L. West. New York: Oxford University Press, 2008.

Homer. *The Iliad*. Translated by Robert Fagles. New York: Penguin, 1998.

Homer. *The Odyssey*. Translated by Robert Fagles. New York: Penguin, 1997.

Horace. *The Complete Odes and Epodes*. Translated by David West. New York: Oxford University Press, 2008.

Ovid. *Metamorphoses*. Translated by A.D. Melville. New York: Oxford University Press, 2008.

Plato. *Symposium*. Translated by Robin Waterfield. New York: Oxford University Press, 2008.

Plutarch. *Essays*. Translated by Robin Waterfield. New York: Penguin, 1992.

Sophocles. *The Complete Plays*. Translated by Paul Roche. New York: Signet, 2010.

Virgil. *The Aeneid*. Translated by Robert Fagles. New York: Penguin, 2010.

Index

CPSIA information can be obtained
at www.ICGtesting.com
Printed in the USA
BVHW050506020323
659519BV00007B/16/J